# Stories Teachers Tell

# Stories Teachers Tell

edited by

GRETCHEN KRESL HASSLER,

with an introduction
and commentary by

JON HASSLER

illustrated by Jerry Fearing

NODIN PRESS

ISBN 1-932472-28-2

We are grateful to all dedicated teachers, who are
the heros of all time. We also thank Jerry Fearing for
his delightful illustrations. And a big thank you to
Norton Stillman for his persistence in getting our
book published.

GKH & JH

Front cover photo: Glenn Hagen
Back cover photo: Judy Olausen

Nodin Press in a division of Micawber's, Inc.
530 N Third Street, Suite 120
Minneapolis, MN 55401

This book is designed for browsing. Open it to any page and you will find a tale from a contemporary classroom, or a school much like the ones my wife Gretchen and I attended fifty years ago, or even a one-room schoolhouse from early in the twentieth century. It's all here, from kindergarten through graduate school; public and private, urban, suburban, and rural; the humorous, the heartbreaking, the inspiring.

We have divided the stories into five sections, beginning with experiences of beginning teachers, those earliest days in the classroom that are marked indelibly in every instructor's memory. Next are a number of success stories, incidents wherein teachers have made a difference in students' lives—or vise versa. This is followed by the opposite sort of story, about failure in the classroom, connections broken and leading, in some cases, to tragedy. Fourth is a lighthearted section, recounting occasions of laughable incidents. Finally we have a section containing two stories so profoundly moving they seem belong in a category of their own—both told, coincidentally, by sisters of the same monastery in St. Joseph Minnesota.

So here's a book for teachers and non-teachers alike, a portrait of those people, who are on hand day after day in our schools and colleges, shaping our next generation of adults.

Jon Hassler

# Table of Contents

## I. STARTING OUT

## II. SUCCEEDING

## III. FAILING

## IV. LAUGHING

## V. TWO MORE STORIES

## Gratitude to the Unknown Instructors

*What they undertook to do*
*They brought to pass;*
*All things hang like a drop of dew*
*Upon a blade of grass.*

W. B. Yeats

# Starting Out

It's been said, by the late Mr. Stephen Humphrey among others, that it's a long mile to a teacher's first classroom. Professor Humphrey taught the Teaching Methods course I attended at St. John's University in the spring of 1955. Not that he taught us very much—we six or eight would-be high school teachers spent most of our time in class diagramming difficult sentences on the blackboard—and yet his style of addressing us was so engaging that I carried it away and used it during my forty-two years as a teacher. It would seem to be a style easy enough to imitate. Simply look your students in the eye and don't lecture, just converse.

But—for a lot of teachers it's not so easy. I discovered quite early in my career that teaching is a skill that can't be taught. My colleagues were either natural teachers or they were never at ease in the classroom. Luckily, I was one of the natural types, for whom teaching came easy. Studying the various faculties I've served on, I've concluded that there are two skills in particular that mark the successful teacher. Apart from a solid grounding in one's subject matter, they are the ability 1) to look people in the eye and 2) to carry on conversations with them. To this day, I believe it's that simple.

I have to add, however, that these two traits will not guarantee perfect discipline in the classroom. Discipline requires firmness and the refusal to smile early in the term. As a beginner, I lost control of more than one class because I wanted to be immediately liked and therefore smiled the first day. Every student will give the teacher the first move. Walk in on any new class and you will see the students pause in their shenanigans, stop their visiting, and turn to look you over. They're taking your measure, wondering what you will be like. This is your opening. Be businesslike at first, stray over to the side of sternness if you must— you can always let up as time goes along—but if you start out easy, you can never bear down.

Good teachers are born, not trained. No matter how many teacher-preparation courses you've taken, it's not until your first year of teaching that you'll know if you're any good at it. Or, as in my own case, your second year—but then, I've always been a slow starter. It was my misfortune to take my first job in a school with a principal who needed to be liked even more than I did. With this man's help I lost control of my first period class. There was in this class a nervous, mouthy high-school junior who seemed unable to shut up and settle down. He wasn't malicious; in fact his manic behavior seemed to grow out of an oversupply of joy, and he would acknowledge each of my reprimands with a sweet, happy smile that I can picture to this day. Let's call him Martin.

Finally, when Martin's behavior began to unsettle the rest of the class, and I was spending more energy quieting the room than I was teaching, I kicked him out. "Go wait in the corridor," I told him, "I'll talk to you after class." It took him a few moments to believe I was serious, and another minute to gather up his books and bid farewell to his friends, but as soon as he was out the door, order was restored. With Martin gone, the class turned its attention to the other incessant speaker in the room—me. But only for about ten minutes. For then the door opened and in walked the principal, leading Martin by the hand.

"What's my friend Martin doing out in the corridor?" he wanted to know, and instead of waiting for me to explain about Martin's incorrigibility, he went on to say that Martin wasn't learning anything out in the hallway this morning. "Take your seat, Martin, it's in here that all the teaching and learning's going on."

The principal left the room as Martin returned triumphantly to his seat, and the class, seeing how easily I had been drained of my authority over them, broke out in excited talk that went on until the end of the term.

Here in this opening section of our book, you are introduced to a number of experienced teachers who, like me, haven't forgotten their earliest days in the classroom.

Jon Hassler

# 1 Making the Grade

Y ou never have to be sorry for what you didn't say."
My mother drummed this into my head at an early
age and it may have helped me hold my tongue at a crucial
moment in the life of a certain ten-year old.

I had been teaching fifth grade in Ridgefield,
Connecticut for about two months when the report card
period ended. Tired as I was on that Sunday evening, I
forced myself to transfer the marks from my record book
to the report cards. Then I decided to break for a cup of
tea. Returning to the task, I inadvertently copied the last
boy's marks into another boy's report card. I continued on
correctly, finishing the cards in time to distribute them at
the close of school the following day.

My fifth grade was mostly made up of average children
with a few very bright and a few rather slow learners, some
of whom could have done better if I could have figured
out the magic needed to motivate them. One of these
was John Morton. John seemed unwilling to sit still very
long, pay attention very long or work independently. His
anecdotal record bore this out, and one after another of
his teachers had dismissed him as immature and hopelessly
unmotivated, with the marks to prove it.

Two days of parent conferences followed the distribution of report cards and I always found it interesting, even surprising, to meet the parents and talk with them individually. When John Morton's young mother came in she greeted me with outstretched hand and the warmest smile. "Mrs. Miller, I'm so glad to meet you!" she enthused. "I can't tell you how thrilled we were with John's report card. I CRIED when I saw it. John's father is on a business trip but I phoned him to tell him about it and of course he was so happy."

She ran on in her talkative way, telling me about John's babyhood, his early childhood, his troublesome younger brother and sister, his difficulties with all his previous teachers, never pausing to notice my complete astonishment. Her twenty minutes were soon over, interrupted by the arrival of the next parent. Mrs. Morton squeezed my hand warmly. Then off she went, leaving me completely bewildered and not a little uneasy. What was she talking about?

The first thing I did when classes resumed was to collect the report cards and examine John's marks. It became clear that I had given John the same excellent marks as Bobby Martin on the line above him in my record book. Fortunately no one had been given John's marks. That fateful break for a cup of tea must have been the explanation. Now what was I to do? Report it to the principal? Call John's mother and tell her it was all a mistake? Offer my apologies to John? Offer my resignation to the school board?

As I often did when I was stymied, I went across the hall to ask the advice of older, wiser, witty and cynical Don Oberon. Years of wrestling with bureaucratic paper work and meager salary increases had given Don a jaundiced view of parents, teachers and certainly administration. He listened with a slight smile, rolling his eyes at my description of my conference with Mrs. Morton. What seemed like a major problem to me was quickly put into perspective.

"Explain what? Are you kidding? Say NOTHING!" advised my mentor. I decided to take his advice. It happened to coincide with my mother's maxim. I hurried back to my room across the hall.

In my class that morning was a complete stranger named John Morton. No more the boy who dawdled with his assignment and talked ceaselessly with his neighbor, John was suddenly tall in his seat, eyes alert, the first to get out his text, the first to begin his work. He was suddenly seeing himself as a completely new person—a success, a scholar, the pride of his parents, a serious student—it was absolutely amazing!

This was not just a nine-day wonder. It continued all year. In fact John's school work improved significantly as did his marks, which only reflected his hard work and new work attitudes. That incident helped me to really understand the importance of self-esteem in children. The only thing I did for John was to keep my mouth shut.

Irene E. Miller
Minnetonka, Minnesota

# 2 The Brilliant Student

*If God speaks French, God thinks in German.*

I was a hot-shot theologian, just back from doctoral studies in Germany, with my head full of footnotes and obscurities, the mark of high German scholarship: "if it is not impenetrable, it is superficial." I was offering a graduate course on the theological nature of the church, and was grading research papers. I came across one paper which was so clear, so perceptive, so highly nuanced, betraying an astonishing theological background, and, above all, an ease of moving organically from one theological area to another, that I came to the conclusion that the paper could not possibly have been written by even a brilliant graduate student. I asked the student—I will call him Mr. Jones—to come to my office, where I confronted him with my conviction that he had plagiarized the paper. He blanched, a sure sign of guilt. Nonetheless, Mr. Jones insisted that he had indeed written the paper himself. I asked to see his notes, which he immediately produced. Beyond doubt the paper was his. I ate crow, apologized, and gave him an A+. Mr. Jones went on to become Professor Jones, a highly successful university professor in another part of the country.

We have never been close.

Kilian McDonnell, OSB
Collegeville, Minnesota

# 3  Picking Winners

After meeting the first class of my teaching career, I told my wife that I had a great-looking student who'd make a terrific date for her sister, who had recently started her first year at the College of St. Benedict. I added that the fellow wouldn't amount to much as an artist, given the fact that his highest aspiration was to "learn to paint bigger and better ducks."

One could not over-estimate the demoralizing impact this modest vision had on me. My enthusiasm to introduce the avant-garde world of twentieth century art was nearly crushed. Imagine, "Bigger and better ducks."!

Favoring loftier issues and aesthetic principles I chose to ignore this young student's desires and teach him what I thought he needed to know.

About fifteen years later I picked up the *Minneapolis*

*Tribune's* "Sunday Magazine." There on the cover was a photo of my student holding the painting which had won for him the Minnesota Duck Stamp Competition. The article explained how fame and fortune were to be his

forever since prints of his painting would be sold in wild-life galleries all across the world. It also quoted his response to an interviewer to the effect that he did not learn much about art in college.

I did arrange a date between this student and my sister-in-law.  It didn't "catch on" either!

Gordon Goetemann
Gloucester, Massachusetts

# 4 Teacher Education

I had always thought that the teacher colleges taught you what you needed to know to be a good teacher.  After all, they called it teacher training. I soon discovered as a new teacher (back in the early sixties), that it wasn't quite the case. It wasn't that the history and philosophy and statistics courses were uninteresting.  If you had a good prof (and some of mine were) and if they could relate the material to the classroom, well, it *was* interesting. But later when I was in the classroom I found that it wasn't enough. Teaching is more art than science, and you have to do art to be an artist. You need teaching-art critics, too. But in education they are usually other experienced teachers.

I began my teaching career in an inner city high school teaching all levels of math. For the college prep classes, the department chair pressed copies of the "new math" textbooks into my hands and wished me good luck.

I had not been exposed to the new math in my college classes, where "cookbook" methods which emphasized doing and not understanding had served me well, so for these classes, I found myself only a page or two ahead of my students.

General math, thank God, was still general math, as it has always been since the time of Archimedes, and that couldn't be too hard to teach, could it? Well it could, and it was. Not because I couldn't do arithmetic, but because half the class knew the material already, and should have been in Algebra, but were too lazy. The other half, ever since grade school, never could count to twenty with their shoes and socks on. But the accepted thinking then, as now in far too many classrooms, was to give them lots more of the same: examples, worksheets, board work, homework, tests and retests. . . .and they still didn't know how to do something like long division.

Joe was one of my students in General Math 10 and Joe was one who, after six years, still didn't get long division. He was a sweet little guy with a smile as wide as his eyes. He sat in the front of the room, near my desk, and was the kind of kid whose job it is to keep the teacher happy. He'd always raise his hand and ask for a more detailed explanation, always trying to avoid being pressed into giving one. He laughed a lot at my lame jokes and seemed to accept the fact that he wasn't very good at math—and that was OK as long as he kept trying.

One day we were doing the same old long division problems. For those who now do these computations only on their calculators, let me remind you that this is a fairly challenging procedure, largely because you have to estimate how many times the divisor goes into the dividend, correctly multiply back and correctly subtracting (bringing down the next digit) and repeating the procedure until the remainder is less than the divisor. At least that's how I learned it. Imagine my surprise as I walked about the room (as a good, young teacher is supposed to do) and looking down at Joe's paper, I saw the following:

$$
\begin{array}{r}
\overline{\phantom{87}} \\
26)\,87 \\
\underline{-26} \\
61 \\
\underline{-26} \\
35 \\
\underline{-26} \\
9
\end{array}
$$

So, we have 26 three times and a remainder of nine. The answer, then, is 3 remainder 9....

"Wow!" I said, "Joe, that's the right answer." Sure enough, he had subtracted the divisor from the dividend until the remainder was less than the divisor. You count up the number of times you subtract it and attach the remainder. Actually, Joe's method is similar to how computers (and calculators) do division. But I hadn't had my lesson from Joe completed until he told me why he did it this way. "My fourth grade teacher saw I couldn't do long division the right way, so she suggested this way." Big Lesson Number One for the new teacher: If at first you don't succeed, and you don't succeed again, see if you can find another way. The next decade would have called it "Different Strokes." Good teachers help their students find a way to do it.

The second lesson, my greatest lesson, also came from Joe. It was several months later when winter winds its way into the tedium of teaching. When you give your class a test and plot their scores, it turns out to look like the McDonald's sign—a large, sloping, capital M. Half the class gets it and half doesn't get it. So, the teacher is forced to come up with some strategies to address the fact that when a new lesson is presented and an assignment is given, half the class is done before the hour is over and the other half may need days to get the work done. My strategy was to bring in extra-credit problems, puzzles, anything that might occupy the mind of a math-hating adolescent by clothing the mathematical concepts in some fuzzy-fun things to do. It isn't easy. As educational author John Holt reminds us, kids are great "crap-detectors."

One mother-lode of good and interesting math puzzles could be found each month in Martin Gardner's math puzzle column in *Scientific American*. That month I lucked across his column on the Soma Cube, the forerunner to the Rubik's Cube. There were a couple of hundred ways to put the pieces together to form the large cube. Of course, there were gazillions of ways it wouldn't go together.

"It's not so hard to do," I said to my class. "Here's one way to put it back together." I fumbled with the pieces as I tried to recall the one solution I had memorized late the night before. To no avail. I put the cube down on the desk of the student I was standing next to as I said, "Well, we're short of time right now. I'm sure you'll figure it out rather easily." Before I could get all those words out of my mouth, the cube, all put together, was rising up into my peripheral vision. The hand holding it was Joe's and I heard his words, "Are there any other puzzles you'd like me to do, Mr. King?"

It turned out that long-division-challenged Joe was a sort of spatial genius. He solved most of Mr. Gardner's more challenging puzzles, too. Joe taught me the Big Lesson Number Two: almost everybody does something very well. Joe did puzzles very well, as I subsequently found out. He had taught me so well that I went out of my way to find more things that more students could do well who had never done very well before. This was long before some educational pundit had coined the term "multiple intelligences." While Joe didn't have much in numerical ability, he was outstanding in spatial and off the charts in infecting other people with his smiles.

I wish I could tell you that I knew what happened to Joe later on. I gave him credit of course. But I'd like to think that he got a job as a draftsman or became a professional on the Soma Cube Tour. I really don't know. The nice thing about Joe was that he was affable, and accepted himself. More importantly, though, I realized he was committed to learning whatever he could.

Joe, I hope you are still out there learning. You sure taught this teacher the importance of staying at it. It's wonderful, isn't it, that each fall, we teachers get another chance to go back into our classrooms with a new group of students and try to learn to be better teachers. September is coming. Happy New Year!

Tom King
St. Paul, Minnesota

# 5 The Milk of 20 Cows

In 1945 when I graduated from St. Cloud State Teacher's College, jobs were a dime a dozen. Superintendents were at the college interviewing students continually. I opted for a job teaching first and second grades in a small town fourteen miles from home.

Two days before school started in the fall, we met with the superintendent. He told me I would be teaching thirty-six six- and seven-year-olds, I would coach GAA (Girls' Athletic Association), spend two hours a week supervising the library, and that I would be expected to monitor one hour a week of high school study-hall. This was not so bad, I could handle it. After all, I was making $1500.00 per year, which came to $131.75 per month after taxes.

All went well until the first session of study hall. Suddenly facing me in a long narrow room were approximately forty students, all waiting with eager eyes to see just how far they could go with a naive twenty-year-old. In my short dress and a pair of anklets and saddle shoes, I took my position at the desk and stared out at all those faces. Everyone was talking, laughing and joking. I banged the ruler on the desk, announcing in my best school-teacher voice, which was not very well established yet, (but which after thirty-five years in the profession has become a doozy): 'THIS IS A STUDY HALL!!" Little response, more noise. From somewhere back in those student teaching sessions I remembered a mentor saying, "Come down hard on the first one that acts up and you will establish control."

One of the senior boys, 6'1", with a devilish grin, who had a pencil up each nostril and one in each ear, became my target. I yelled, he answered, the pencils jiggled, the study hall burst with laughter, and I lost my temper (which has always been fierce) and announced, "OK, you're staying after school!"

"I can't, I ride the bus." The pencils jiggled some more—more laughter—more anger.

"I could care less, you can walk home!"

An iffy silence from the room, the pencils were removed, and in a meeker voice, "I got chores on the farm."

I'd gone too far to back down now. "That's your problem, not mine, and that goes for anyone else who chooses to play games."

School closed, the buses left, and David and I sat. Make this good, I thought, so we sat until 5:00 P.M.

Walking back to my rooming house, I was tired, hungry, discouraged, and wondering what the next day would bring. Just as I walked in the door, my landlady said, "Here she is now" and handed me the phone.

I barely said hello before the voice on the other end said, "Who do you think you are, keeping my kid until 5 o'clock? We milk twenty cows." This was followed by a few more choice words before I could get a word in. When I did, I thought, well, so much for the teaching profession, because I can't promise not to repeat my performance should David become disruptive again.

However, as I took my desk the next time we had that study hall, there was utter silence. What I couldn't do with a banging ruler, one angry father had done when he had to milk all 20 cows.

Florence Birkemeyer Evans
Lake Crystal, Minnesota

# 6  The Art of Teaching

I became a teacher by default: nobody could think of anything else to pursue when I turned into an awkward teenager. World War II had just ended. British troops had moved over the mountain-passes from Northern Italy. The Cossack army, which had surrendered to the British, had been handed over to the Soviets and executed. Their horses were smoked to sausages in the wood-fired smokestacks of the idyllic farm houses in the Lesach Valley high up in the Carnic Range of the Alps. My father had also been a teacher, but he was missing in action somewhere in Yugoslavia. Ten years later, he would be declared dead.

Meanwhile, my mother had to fend for four children. Away from home, I was working as a farm-hand with a local farmer way up in the mountains between Carinthia and Friuli, thus providing some food and scant income, but certainly no future.  Graduating from high-school was marked with an all-day hike on the Gerlitze, a mountain with a spectacular view of the neighboring peaks. "Make sure you hand in your application to the teacher-training college before the day is over," my mother said firmly, because she knew what would be the best for me. In fact, it was the only thing she could think of, while waiting for her husband's return, which never happened. So, I wrote an application on the train during the stops, when the shaking and bumping ceased briefly, and mailed it at the last train-station. It was not a polished document.

The five-year institution I attended was eager to produce a young generation of teachers because most of the older ones were either POWs or civil servants and thus members of the Nazi Party. Before the first class of the young generation was graduated, however, the old comrades were pardoned and re-employed, thus eliminating the need for young teachers, who were considered unemployable, inexperienced, and unneeded. I found employment as a tutor for retarded children. I also was a decent clarinet player and made a living playing at dances on weekends. And I played the organ during masses on Sundays, for which I got a free meal in the local inn. Would I ever be able to use in class what I had learned?

What I did remember was the fatherly voice of a methods teacher, who was also a decent writer: "When you teach, you must love your students, and you must love the things you teach. Everything else will fall into place."

In winter 1953, a sick-leave in some forsaken village way up in the Alps provided me with a temporary teaching position. I walked for three hours past the last train-stop and reached the village, my belongings in a heavy rucksack. Next morning, a middle-aged principal, who taught grades 5 to 8 in a classroom smelling of sweat, smoke, and old clothes, introduced me to the pupils in grade one to four, also smelling of sweat, smoke, and unwashed clothes. "Make sure they know how to read and write in first grade before the end of the year," she said. And that was about the last instruction I received prior to my premiere as a country school teacher.

But how does one teach students how to read and write, let alone all the other things referred to rather generically in fading lesson plans made up by colleagues long retired or dead? There were hardly any textbooks. All the books with Nazi references were used as heating materials, but there were politically neutral art supplies, and lots of paint. Not just brown, but also yellow and blue, green and pink, gold and black. There were stacks of wrapping paper. I found brushes. From now on, there was no day when I didn't paint with my pupils in the manner of the Fauves: Wild and wonderful. Big and bold. Shedding all inhibitions and reservations. Every day a feast for this artist-colony otherwise used to cleaning out barns and herding sheep. I loved their displays of agony and ecstasy. I loved their explosions of creativity. I loved their bold strokes—and I loved my kids, who loved me because I was such a strange guy. Most of all, they loved me because they did not have to do much writing, reading, and arithmetic. I simply let them paint. And paint they did. Some of their finest achievements I took to my room, where the housekeepers thought I did these strange "modern" things myself, and thought I was weird. Every day was colorful and exciting.

In May, the state-inspector came to ascertain the success—or lack thereof—of the young, struggling teacher. He was appalled when he noted the absence of expertise in the three Rs in grades one to four. He took no consolation from the fact that the walls were full of works that could have graced a modern gallery. I decided that life as a country school teacher may not be the thing to pursue. I left the remote valley and took a position as an instructor for drawing and design at a vocational school for engravers, gunsmiths, and tool-and-die makers.

Otmar M. Drekonja
Collegville, Minnesota

# 7 The Silent E

Some of today's kids are so precocious. I had to be a sophomore in high school, a wise moron, before I realized that no male should tell anyone he likes poetry.

As a poet-in-residence in the public schools, I have a fill–in-the-blank game I ask elementary students to play by way of warming them up for more serious poems. It's a simple device of having them write themselves inside anything they wish.

Once, after writing two or three of these, a fourth-grade boy went into something I thought impossible for his age:

> *I am inside a poem.*
> *I am inside the p.*
> *It is noisy in here.*
> *I am inside the o.*
> *It is quiet in here.*
> *I an inside the e.*
> *There is not a thing going on in here.*
> *I am inside the m.*
> *I feel good in here.*

Some people may like their miracles larger. I don't. And has anyone ever written a better description of the silent e?

But it was the last line of his poem which foreshadowed what this fourth grader would tell me at the end of the week. He came up when I was eating my first flying saucer (warm minced ham topped with mashed potatoes and melted cheese) and said, "Don't tell anybody, but I like poetry. It makes me feel good."

Don Welch
Kearney, Nebraska

# 8  I Smiled in December

I learned in mid-August, 1958, that I would be teaching World History and English to sophomores, Civics to juniors, and U. S. History to seniors five days a week. I think I was in a state of denial for several days. (This can't be happening to me. I don't like history. I got Ds in history in grade and high school and I've had only one semester of government. Why me, Lord?) When reality set in, I was so overwhelmed that I could not concentrate on lesson plans, class projects or anything I should have been preparing for my first semester in the classroom. Instead, I spent time creating clever bulletin boards and neatly writing the names of my students in the bright red spiral-bound grade book I was given.

That year Ottumwa Heights Academy was housed in an empty instruction building at an abandoned naval air base, because our motherhouse and school burned to the ground in a disastrous fire on October 8, 1957. The city of Ottumwa had provided us with living quarters and teaching facilities at the air base until we could rebuild. The old instruction building had been used for grain storage, so each morning we would check (and empty!) the dozen or more mouse-traps that had been set the night before.

I had learned all the "new teacher commandments": be strict; be stern; show confidence; demand attention; and don't smile in the classroom for at least the first three months. I had those rules down pat.

At 1:10 on the dreaded Tuesday afternoon, I walked into my third class of the day, junior Civics, already exhausted from having met with sophomores for World History at 10 AM, and that same group of forty girls for English at 11 o'clock. Would I make it through this class and then yet another at 2:10?

As I had done in the morning, I planned to devote the entire fifty-minute period to giving these eager students an overview of the course. Frankly, I figured this gave me another day to prepare to actually "teach" them something.

I had written a brief outline, consisting mostly of the chapter titles of the textbook, and I talked for a minute or two about each of these (mostly just lifting one idea from the chapter). I got to the topic of immigration (chapters 14 and 18) and told the class that we would spend a few days examining the Immigration Laws of 1952. Of course, at that point I didn't know anything about those laws. But we wouldn't get to those for several weeks so I had time to study the material.

Suddenly a hand went up—the first of the day! Glory be to God, what do I do now? "Yes," I said, remembering to maintain my stern countenance.

"Sister, would you comment on our present quota system? Is it fair?" Then another hand went up "Do you think we should allow more people from Asia into our country?"

Having no idea whether these kids were knowledgeable about the immigration laws or just "testing" the new teacher, I froze. I couldn't discuss quota system with them. I didn't know anything about the quota system. I wanted to scream, "Hey, kids, that's not fair. That doesn't come until much later in the textbook. Give me a break."

Finally, after asking the first hand-raiser her name, I said, "Well, Ann, I haven't given that much thought yet. Why don't you tell us what you think about the quota system?"

The rest of the class period turned into a lively discussion about the U. S. immigration policy, what should be changed and why. I just stood and listened.

I left that classroom feeling I had failed. I went to the teachers' lounge and told Sister Carol, a veteran Spanish teacher, my tale of woe. I didn't ever want to see that class again. Sister gave me a few words of encouragement and sent me off to my U. S. History class. Fortunately for me, no hands went up in that class.

At 1:10 the next day I was facing those same thirty-seven junior girls, wondering, as they stared up at me, just what they really knew about U. S. government. I had burned the midnight oil reading about immigration and quota systems. But to what avail? Every girl in that room sensed that I knew little about government. They would probably ask me about foreign diplomacy or trade negotiations, these being among the many topics I still had to bone up on. But they didn't challenge me. In fact, I soon discovered that Ann, Patty, and several of the others were bright, inquisitive, imaginative students and they were a tremendous help to me in getting through that first semester of teaching.

Many years later, long after I was assigned to administration duties, I had a visit with Ann, the girl who wanted me to comment on the quota system. We chuckled about that first day of class and we decided that we learned a lot from each other that year. Ann even reminded me that before the end of the semester, I had put on a happy smile!

Dolores Schuh, CHM
Collegeville, Minnesota

# 9  Opening Up

E ach morning, before the bells begin ringing, I unlock my classroom door and enter, like an old shopkeeper whose rituals are the currency of neighborhood conversation. I switch on the lamps, tune the radio to a station the kids will object to, allow my glance to rest briefly here, then here around the room. . . But these are not the habits of an old man. Like the Navajo silversmith who pauses at his tools, humble before the unworked metal, to chant his thanks, I have done the same since the first day. . .

And each of these days is the day before a parade when the floats stand poised in some somber garage; a glow like the one that surrounds rising bread dough in a warm corner of the kitchen, and the golden smell of something like yeast nearby.

The chairs under the tables dream of standing up and becoming great writers, statesmen, actors. The books repose on their shelves like those sharks discovered sleeping and docile by *National Geographic* photographers.

George Roberts
Minneapolis, Minnesota

# Succeeding

One of the teachers in this section says, "When I am out of sorts with my colleagues and all I've come to, I know that when I enter the classroom, where I close the door and begin to talk and question, I have returned to one of the great solaces of my life. "

He is the poet Jay Meek and he teaches at the University of North Dakota in Grand Forks. He also claims that we ought to "give our final exams on the first class of the semester, to find out what we know and do not know. The last class we need to reserve for cheer and sadness—that we as a party have ventured deep into poems, and will not go this way together again."

I know what he means. Meeting your students in the classroom feels like setting out on a journey, and then, when the term ends and the class disbands, you realize that you will never again be able to duplicate this experience. For each class has a distinct personality. From my forty-two years of teaching I remember classes that were rowdy, silent, sleepy, eager, clever, slow to catch on, fun-loving, defiant, complicated, compliant, witty, and so forth—no two precisely alike, yet each one memorable and fascinating to work with. And I remember the thrill of witnessing the opening of a mind in the classroom, sometimes a student's mind, sometimes my own. Unfortunately, as in the story "Joshua," the mind will sometimes open for only a moment, then close again, but more often, as in "Making the Grade," it will open for a lifetime.

In this chapter we meet a number of teachers who obviously agree that it is this mind-opening experience, with its never-ending parade of personalities, both individual and combined, that makes teaching such a vital and interesting vocation.

Jon Hassler

# 10  Notes of a Teaching Poet

I don't believe the writing of poetry or fiction can be taught, although I'm equally sure it has to be learned. All of us, for good or ill, are instructors, and I know that I've learned almost as much from teaching as from being taught. I've learned from poems and poets, learned more than I know, forgotten more than I can say. At lunch hour, in love with contraries, I go out searching for a delicate delicatessen.

*

As a student, I wrote short stories with a teacher who had been a carnival worker. We all loved him for it. Sitting in his office on a fall day in Ann Arbor, with mist blowing across the quadrangle, I listened to him remark on my story. I'd written something dull and I didn't know how to fix it. He stood at the window and looked out into the funk. There was no reproof or condescension in his voice. He said I needed a fire truck in it. He didn't blink. I didn't question. But since that day I've tried to set at least one fire in whatever I've written.

*

One of the most unyielding aspects of any job is how little it gives us to learn. As a teacher, I consider myself lucky to go on learning, get paid for reading poems, and be with people who are in good health and beautiful and curious and young. That's something, isn't it?

*

I believe we should give our final exams on the first class of the semester, to find out what we know and do not know. The last class we need to reserve for sadness and cheer, that we have come up short, that we who as a party have ventured far into poems will not go this way together again.

*

On days when I am out of sorts with colleagues and all I've come to, I know that when I enter the classroom, when I close the door and begin to talk and question, I have returned to one of the great solaces of my life.

Jay Meek<br>Grand Forks, North Dakota

# 11  Truth or Fiction

Joyce Carol Oates' fine short story, "Where Are You Going, Where Have You Been?" features Connie, a summary of the negative stereotype of a fifteen-year-old.

This young woman is shallow, taken with the values of her peer culture, and headed for a disastrous end. The story generally provides an opportunity to talk about malls and music, superficiality and popular culture, so I expected a stimulating class one day when I stood arranging my notes on the podium and my students settled into their desks. Then I noticed one particular young man sitting there weeping. I could sense the atmosphere change in the room as his peers began to notice his teary eyes. It grew very quiet. Wondering what to do about him—perhaps he should leave the room?—I gave him a questioning look. He pointed toward Oates' story and said, "This is my sister."

Class having been taught, I had only to say, "Class dismissed."

W. Dale Brown
Grand Rapids, Michigan

## 12 Blessings

One morning in October 1982, I was called to sub at Spalding, a public school for mentally and physically handicapped children in Chicago. I didn't know what kind of school Spalding was until I got there and saw the kids on the playground. What I saw were kids in wheelchairs, kids wearing leg braces, kids sporting mechanical arms or legs, and kids wearing spinal injury helmets. However, just like any group of kids on a playground in the morning before school starts, these kids were bustling about playing football, playing tag, sharing homework, and generally just trying to make the most of the last few minutes before the bell rang.

I am assigned to the new wing. It is for pre-school-age kids, and I find myself in a large, blue-carpeted room with two aides and one teacher. The teacher is a gentle-eyed woman named Mary with slightly graying, short black hair. Mary is the master teacher in charge of this unit. She wears a blue denim skirt and a blue-and-white striped button-down cotton shirt. There are only a few kids on the floor making attempts at play. I'm wondering where the other students are.

Mary and the aides leave and one of the physical therapists wheels in a young boy about four. He is strapped into what looks like a high chair on wheels except that he is standing. The straps are secured around his calves, his waist and his chest. His arms rest on the tray of the high chair-like contraption, and his head is held in place by one of those helmet-like wire frames without the shell of the helmet that are used for people with spinal injuries.

Not feeling very useful to this point, I pick up one of

those plastic toy squares with geometrically-shaped holes in the sides, into which a child can put plastic pieces by matching the shape of the piece with the shape of the hole. It's a large motor, hand-eye activity that also teaches shape. I go over to the boy, who is cute as a button. He has olive skin and thick, curly black hair, curly as only the hair of a child can be. I place the toy in front of him and begin to show him how to play. I drop a star in the star hole, a half moon in the half moon hole, and so on. He doesn't respond at all. His arms and hands remain motionless on the tray of his contraption.

I pick up one of the pieces, the circle, and try to place it in his right hand. His little fingers remain limp, and the circle falls onto the tray. I try to help him wrap his fingers around the circle by squeezing them around it, but my fingers are doing all the grasping. His just don't respond. I reach over and bring the square towards us, lifting his right hand up to meet the appropriate cutout side. I open my hand and let the circle piece fall. It falls onto the square but misses the circle slot and tumbles off the toy, bounces on the tray and falls to the ground. I set the little boy's hand back down on the tray and retrieve the fallen piece.

Mary returns and walks over to help me out. She smiles at me kindly and then at the boy. She begins tussling with the straps on his contraption in order to loosen them and says, "Probably the best thing for him is to let him out of this thing for awhile." She finishes undoing the straps around his calves and then takes hold of him under his armpits from behind. She motions for me to undo the rest of the straps. I do and then she manages, while still holding him up, to extricate him from his helmet. I look on, feeling absolutely helpless. My stomach actually turns over in sadness. I feel myself wanting to cry, but I don't.

Mary hauls the boy up out of his high chair, walks over to where there is a rubber mat, and lays him down on his stomach. She strokes his side a few times and coos, "There you go. That feels better now doesn't it?" The boy just kind of wobbles on his belly like a fish, his head flopping around. But his eyes kind of roll up at her as if to thank her for releasing him. I think he smiles as much as he can, which is really no more than a quiver of his lips. Then his expression falls and he is left to wobble and roll, occasionally moving slightly in what appears to be an attempt at a whole body stretch. He begins uttering a very low groan and drooling at the mouth.

Mary tells me that he is one of the less fortunate ones. His parents gave him up to a home from which he is bussed in every day. They rarely visit him, having been unable, over time, to deal with his condition, which I can't remember the name for but which causes him to have little or no control over his muscles. He probably won't live long, she tells me. It's a terminal condition. "There really isn't much you can do for him," she says.

I realize then that we are caring for the dying here,

those for whom pleasure consists in being laid on the ground and allowed to simply rest, free of the various devices used to hold them up and move them about. Later, towards the end of the day, Mary offers me a cadre position, but I turn it down. I feel terrible saying no, but I know that I couldn't do it.

It is raining that day when I leave the school. A heavy, steady rain, but I walk the few miles to my apartment because I feel like it. I feel like walking so that I can feel all of the muscles in my body, from my head down to my toes, move inside of me. I feel like walking so that I can feel the firmness of the pavement on the soles of my feet and the way my hand wraps around and grips hold of the smooth, solid, plastic handle on my umbrella. I walk all the way home that day, and all the way home I watch the rain fall steadily down around me. All the way home I watch the drops that fall from the tips of the frame of my small umbrella. All the way home I feel the tears roll down my cheeks thinking about the kids at Spalding, but all the way home I think how good it is, how damn good it is, to walk all the way home.

Craig Kirsch
Chicago, Illinois

# 13 The First Day of Creation

Eda Kriseova, in *Vaclav Havel: The Authorized Biography*, says of the Czech Republic playwright and president, one of my heroes, that "everything interests and astonishes him as if he had just seen it for the first time." I hope this can be said of me. If it can, it's partly because of a lesson about teaching I learned years ago from my students.

Teaching a Bible course at Swarthmore College, I was generally successful at getting and sustaining attention even though we met first period in the morning. One term, however, the fire didn't catch. There wasn't rebellion, but there was resistance. Had I lost the gift? After a few weeks of frustration, I asked a few of the students to come to my office to talk. I don't remember how I introduced the question. It was probably enveloped by a smokescreen of academic indirection. But its gist was simple: "Help!"

What they said stunned me, because it meant that what I was doing to make the class come alive was killing it.

"You begin most class sessions by saying, 'As I was going over the material for today, I noticed for the first time—this or that.'" They were generous-spirited enough to acknowledge my good motive: I wanted to convey my continuing excitement about my subject. You could work at this stuff for years—I'd been teaching nearly a decade by now—and still not exhaust it, still be surprised by it.

Then the zinger. "You may be seeing something new this go-around, but we've never seen what you saw the first time you looked at it." From that moment I date my recognition of a fundamental truth of teaching: My responsibility is not only, not even mainly, to keep finding new things, but to nurture in myself and others "interest and astonishment about everything," including what I've done over and over again, "as if for the first time."

Every day in the classroom is the first day of creation.

Patrick Henry
Waite Park, Minnesota

# 14  The New Itinerant

One day, in April, I brought David Haynes to come in to talk to students who had read his novel *Right By My Side* in their eighth-grade class. Because he is a former public school teacher himself, David is always an ideal guest. On this day, he had before him 120 students between the ages of 12 and 15. And he waded right in there, asking questions, pulling reactions out of them, responding to their comments.

They were more attentive than I had ever seen them—entertained and absorbed by this man in front of them—and one of the most mesmerized, I noticed as I watched the crowd, was a boy named Tommy. He was a round-faced, round-bodied African American boy who had been teased unmercifully all year long for being too studious, for not being a jock, for not being black enough, for being too smart. His teachers had been encouraging him to hang in there, assuring him that all his studying, all his work, would eventually pay off. And so he did hang in there, asking fine questions, trying all the activities he was assigned, working hard at his studies. On the day of David's visit, he looked positively transcendent. He watched David move around the room, laughed at David's self-deprecating jokes, waited for David to call on him.

Later, after the talk, I saw Tommy again. He was carrying lunches into a classroom where David was to meet with ten selected students for a more intimate talk about writing, reading, and any other questions that came up. I asked Tommy how he was doing, and he answered, "This is the best day I have ever had!" I smiled, excited for him, relieved that David's visit had worked out so well.

It wasn't until I was in my car and heading home that I realized why Tommy was *this* happy, why he looked transformed, beaming, relaxed. It was because, across from him in that lunch room, above him in that auditorium, stood the possibilities for himself. There he was, thirty years down the road: African American, round, with glasses, not liking sports and enjoying language. There in front of Tommy was the validation of all we had tried to tell him: it would pay off some day, he would find those like him in the world.

Julie Landsman
Minneapolis, Minnesota

# 15 Transition

Sometimes the vision of a student is so raw and truthful the art of his writing is almost irrelevant.

For three days I tried to encourage a fifth-grade boy into writing, and he only smiled. I asked his teacher why he wouldn't write, and she told me he never wrote and rarely spoke, so he surprised me by writing a poem the next day. His teacher was dumbfounded. Enlisting the help of a custodian, the elementary principal, and even the school nurse, we tried to decipher it. You can image the handwriting of a boy who had never written anything in school. It was worse than the hieroglyphics on the Rosetta

Stone. Still, in time, this is what we transcribed:

> I am inside my head.
> It is a disaster
> It is all falling apart.
> There are little green men
> Tearing it apart.
> I look out my eye
> I see a sign that says
> Do Not Disturb.

Upon my persistent questioning one teacher finally revealed the boy had been traumatized before he came to school by a drunken father who had thrown children out of the house, even through closed windows.

I took a chance and read the boy's poem to the class the next day. When I finished, he had his head on his desk, and for a moment, I thought I might have sent him back into even more silence. Then I got down onto one knee and looked up into his face. He was smiling. The last day of the week he wrote, "I used to be an old junk car, but now I am a Trans-Am."

Don Welch,
Kearney, Nebraska

## 16 Elaine and Debbie

As a teacher of eighteen years, I have heard people say many times, "Kids are not the same any more." I disagree with this statement. I think kids are the same as they have always been—mixed-up, looking for some direction and often surprisingly strong.

Journal writing. Although studies have proven its effectiveness in the teaching of writing, teachers use it as often as not because it gives them a few blessed moments of quiet to begin class and to take attendance.

One day during journal-writing in a large ninth-grade class, one of my students, Elaine, began to moan softly, then more loudly and coherently: "I can't see, I can't see, I can't see! I Can't See!!" Elaine, who was rather large, with dyed blonde hair and black eye makeup, seemed to be in real distress. The entire class was becoming upset by Elaine's problem and journal writing was being interrupted. I had only been teaching a short time and was unsure how to deal with this sudden case of blindness, so I signaled Steven, one of the more responsible students, to take my stricken student to the office.

After a minute or two, Steven returned. I gave him a questioning look, but he just shrugged. Shockingly, after another five minutes, Elaine returned to class and slipped into her seat as if nothing had happened! Since this was a Catholic school, and the office was located opposite the chapel, I could only suppose that a miracle had occurred to restore the girl's sight. After class I asked Elaine what happened. She merely responded, "I had on too much eye makeup."

I think young people do struggle to succeed these days. Too often these struggles are complicated by family problems and financial problems. These problems provide the basis for the struggle for individual identity that is common to all adolescents.

One student whom I greatly admired was named Debbie. She was a new student at Sheridan, and she was a little quiet. Physically, she was not striking: medium height, honey-blond hair, glasses, brown eyes and a bit heavy. However, I became interested in her because of the consistent quality of the work she turned in.

One day after class I asked her about herself, and she told me her story in remarkably objective terms. She had two sisters. (All three had different fathers.) Her mother had had two children by the time she was eighteen. Debbie was the baby—her mother was nineteen when she was born. Debbie's two sisters had traveled paths similar to her mother's—both were teen mothers themselves, and both were living at home. Neither had completed high school. Debbie took stock of the situation and decided that to avoid the same path, she had to move. She lived at that time in a small town in eastern Colorado. She found a cousin who was willing to allow her to move into her small apartment in Denver. She would sleep on her couch, find a school to attend, and contribute a small amount of rent.

Debbie started in the local Denver public high school, but wanted more of a challenge than the inner city school afforded. She found out that our school district accepted out-of-district students. She figured out how to get to the school by bus. Then she enrolled in our school. She was fifteen at the time.

Once enrolled at Sheridan, Debbie continued to demonstrate her maturity. She maintained a strong B-A average in her classes while working a forty-hour week. She became the first in her family to graduate from high school and to enroll in the university. She is now in her third year of a nursing program. She is living back in the same small town with her mother and sisters, but by reordering her life at the age of fifteen, she put herself on a path to succeed.

Looking at the struggles of students to find identity in a complex world, I generally find myself full of admiration for their successes.

Jeff Mayer
Sheridan, Colorado

# 17  Poetry Lesson

Three weeks left of school,
a hot May day
eighth graders eager
to be launched,
enter—barely at the bell,
go straight to the windows
and open them wide.
Papers swirl from the ledge.
I ask—ready to finish
the year in a flourish—
"What is poetry?"
Jessica—so quiet—always
on the outskirts of any circle—
has notebooks full of poetry,
illustrated in soft pastels.
She's written of her blind father
expertly fingering Braille,
reading Bible stories to her
as she nestles in his lap.
Jessica says, "Poetry is the
closest thing to truth I know."
Monica came to us midyear.
She rarely comes to school.

Stomach aches, her mother says.
She once wrote a two page poem.
I suggest
it is a little vague,
could you be more concrete?
She revises—and I see she has
written a lament to
lost virginity.
Monica says, "Poetry can
Express the innermost feeling
of your soul.
Brian—the class clown—
has a folder full of poems.
He writes metaphors as easily as
he writes his name.
Brian says, "Poetry is
A bunch of phony crap.
It doesn't mean much."
Three weeks left of school—

Eighth graders ready to be launched
sit in a hot classroom—
Studying…Poetry.

Sandy Nesvig
St. Paul, Minnesota

# 18 The Way to the Mind

When staffing cuts got me "demoted" to the junior high after ten years of teaching high school English, my colleagues commiserated over the loss of intellectual stimulation I would suffer among eighth graders. But I soon learned that there were enough emotional compensations to keep me going.

One of my favorites came after the last curtain call of Sandburg Junior High's spring musical, the melodrama *No, No, A Thousand Times No,* which I co-directed with the vocal music teacher. Together we had tailored the script, blocked, choreographed, and trained a cast of fledglings to sing, dance, and act. It had been my first experience as a director, too, and I confess that the end result was far more inspired and inspiring than any of us could have hoped for.

I had just closed the doors on the empty auditorium when one last eighth-grade boy emerged from the side door of the green room. Expecting to see no one, he leapt without looking. He jettisoned down the length of the hallway, clicking his heels first to the left and then to the right, singing out with each leap, "I can dance! I can dance!" His private delight was mine as well.

Shortly thereafter I applied to the Graduate Program in

English at the University of Minnesota, where intellectual stimulation abounds and emotions are buried deeply.

I got the Ph.D. in 1991 and miraculously landed a job at University of Wisconsin-River Falls, where I love watching the changes in the thinking and self-expression between first-semester and second-semester freshmen and where having my own office provides a spot where teacher-student emotions do not have to be entirely repressed. But I do miss the opportunity to direct musicals and to assign skits and role-playing as part of my regular classroom practice. It's not just the bliss of play or self-expression, but the untroubled joy of *amateurism*. My career as a junior high school teacher gave me a lasting insight into my job: You'll never get to the mind with a heart by-pass.

Ruth Wood
River Falls, Wisconsin

# 19  The Millionaire

After teaching for several years I realized that the day before Christmas Vacation (i.e. Winter Break) was not the best teaching day of the year. So, I developed an activity named the "Werschay-o-gram" in which students would answer on paper the twenty questions asked by naming another student in the class. This managed to keep the eighth-graders at North Junior High School in St. Cloud in their desks and somewhat meaningfully occupied.

All of these responses were anonymous and no copying or looking at other student's answers was allowed.  Such questions as "Who do you think is the smartest person in this room?" "If a student in this room became President of the United States thirty-five years from now, who do you think it might be?" "Who do you think is the quietest person in this room?" "Who do you think is the class clown?" etc.

The real fun of this activity was to collect the papers, shuffle them up, and then pass them back to the students for correction. I would repeat each question, and the students would read off the answers that were written on the paper they happened to be correcting. There were smiles, laughs, groans, and some finger pointing, but it was all in good fun, and everyone seemed to walk out of class a little taller.

Perhaps the most memorable moment came one year when I asked a particularly unmotivated class to answer the following question, "If you had a million dollars but you had to give it to someone else in this room, whom would you give it to?" I then told the class to NOT look up from their paper until the answer was written.

As I corrected the papers later the answer given to the millionaire question was invariably the same: "Jenny," "Jen," "Jenny," "Jen," "Jen," "Jenny." EVERY student in the class had selected Jenny. Then all eyes turned to Jenny, a physically handicapped girl, sitting in her wheelchair in the front of the room on the left side.

There are many ups and downs to teaching junior high

school. Whenever things got particularly difficult in later years, I would recall that incident in that room at that moment. It never failed to reinforce my faith in the overall goodness and generosity of junior high students.

Robert E. Werschay
St. Cloud, Minnesota

# 20 Navigating Scylla and Charybdis

One of the classes it has been my good fortune to teach is the high school newspaper journalism class at Armstrong High School. I signed on for what I thought would be a one-year stint while the regular teacher was on sabbatical. When she returned, she clearly signaled her desire to remain on sabbatical from newspaper advisorship and journalism classroom teaching, so I good-naturedly agreed to continue. Besides, I liked the kids.

The students produced articles and special reports that the nodding and napping ones would wake up to read. Their efforts paid off, and by the second year I served as journalism teacher and advisor, we noted that the entire school population was uncharacteristically alert but quiet during homeroom on distribution day. Instead of sleeping or chatting, the students were reading our paper.

And so we produced issue after issue, working hard to create punchy, attention-getting leads, inviting controversy, and winning journalism awards with frank coverage of teenage pregnancy, abortion rights, the Gulf War, classroom censorship, civil liberties in school and out, student-installed, battery-powered fish tanks, burglar alarms in lockers, dress codes, and violence in the school. With rare exceptions, we stayed out of trouble and avoided trips to the principal's office. Then, along came AIDS, condoms, and "safe" sex.

This was the early 1990s, after all, and HIV/AIDS was a major concern for heterosexuals as well as homosexuals, *Odyssey* reporters said. The editors launched a campaign to cover all aspects of the matter. The first topic listed on their idea sheet was "protected sexual encounters" (they loved discussing condoms in serious, journalistic fashion). Among article ideas were nudity in museum art and on swimming beaches around the world, homosexuality, teen romance, and sex education in health classes. Their "fair and balanced coverage" goal was to research teenage sexuality in as many variations as possible. My goal was to keep my job so I could continue to make house payments. I said as much, and they responded with sly smiles and, "Oh, Ms. Williams, just relax. We're responsible. Look at our work so far."

"That's just my point," I responded.

"And think of the awards we'll win," they threw in, knowing my weak spot.

"Safer sex, because that's what it is, not safe sex like so many people think," said Marcy, whose father is a biologist. "So it can be a teen health issue. We can even run instructions on how to use condoms, what can happen if one breaks, for example, maybe an illustration of how to put one on." I blanched.

Deadline day arrived for reading first drafts of leads. I noticed the sex section sitting together on my left, so I started on the right side of the room with sports. Predictably, their leads were full of high hopes and smashed opponents. After sports, news, the sex group showed signs of restlessness, so we turned to them next. Entertainment and movie reviews might have to wait until the next day.

The class sat back in their chairs, little fires igniting in their eyes. The spectacle they had all been waiting for was about to begin. I hadn't fooled any of them with the weak warm-up show. They had come expecting heavy metal and a brawl. Anticipation ran high. Censorship. Blood on the rug. Battles royal. Then, before I could use up any more valuable time stalling and sermonizing about responsible journalism, the nude beach/nude art reporter waved her hand. "Let me start, Ms. Williams, I have the best lead, you'll love it."

"Good taste?" I asked. "We have a captive audience here."

"Absolutely," she said. I studied her smile, then nodded. She held out her paper, paused dramatically, then intoned, "All men have penises and all women have vaginas." She lowered the paper. I blinked. The eyes in the classroom moved as a single organism and watched

me. "That's a fact," she said triumphantly, "and you can't deny it. It could be in a health textbook it's so factual. No censorship, right?"

I nodded, looked at the floor a split instant, then swung my head up and answered. "You're absolutely right.

You've written the facts, and I wouldn't censor the facts you present. But the lead you've written, well, it's not news. You've stated what have been facts for practically forever. Nothing new or exciting there. Above all else, we're a newspaper, and leads need to trumpet the news." Then I grinned. I had saved myself, the class knew I had saved myself, and my relief was palpable.

She stared at me a moment, the class watched, then she gestured helplessly, a funny little smile on her face. She wasn't going to fight this one. The built-up tension had no where else to go, and we all burst out laughing. My humanitarian sports reporter gave me a thumbs up, then we moved on. No unseemly gloating, no restating the obvious. Just news leads, catchy and timely.

The students went on to produce a high-spirited, lively paper chock-full of facts. Hardly anyone threw that issue of the newspaper on the floor or in the wastebaskets after homeroom on distribution day. My house payment was safe, at least until the next issue.

Lorna Williams
Minneapolis, Minnesota

# 21 One Small Act

Every year we have dress-up days at our school for homecoming week. Fridays are always reserved for school spirit day. Some students dress up in school colors and team uniforms. Some even color their hair. They do almost anything to show their school spirit.

I always joined the students in dressing up, and this day was no different. A half hour before school was to start I was sitting at my desk applying some finishing touches of paint to my face when a student walked in. Her name was Rhoada, and she was a girl with special needs.

Rhoada was very friendly but very lonely. She walked with a slight limp, spoke with a slur, and had a very difficult time learning. I could tell she was concentrating on my face paint. "Rhoada," I said to her, "would you like your face painted?"

Her face instantly exploded into a smile. Although I simply painted a D-C on one cheek and a '97 on the other, she responded as if it was the biggest gift of her life. She walked out of my room that morning with her head higher than I had ever seen it before. Later in the day, I saw her pointing her face paint out to other students and teachers. It was as if she felt a part of the school for the first time.

For the next year after that homecoming Friday,

Rhoada often poked her head into my room as she passed by, and she always had that same smile on her face.

Rhoada graduated the next year, but I still think about all the thirty-second meetings people have in a day. I marvel at how an act that took about thirty seconds of my time could have had such a large impact. It was like a rock tossed into pond. The splash soon passes, but the ripples billow out long afterward, washing other rocks on other shores.

Paul Beckermann
Dassel, Minnesota

# 22 Walk in Another Man's Zonis

As the first director (1961) of the Institute of American Studies at the East West Center of the University of Hawaii, my job was to devise schemes for explaining America to Asian students and visitors. Our first "mission" was to debrief a group of Indian journalists who were about to go on an extended visit to the Mainland. We tried to imagine what they would want to know. We thought it prudent to prepare ourselves to deal with the usual litany of American errors: racism, materialism, isolationism,

Disney superficiality. After bringing our grueling seminar in self-recrimination to a close, we dispersed, ready to greet those Brown Indians on the morrow.

But a funny thing happened on the way to our first cross-cultural confrontation. The Indian journalists didn't want to ask us embarrassing questions about our hastily assembled self-indictment. The first question they asked was: Why do you treat your old people so cruelly?

Huh? We were of that first generation of American parents who wouldn't think of inflicting themselves on our kids. And we had grown up thinking of grandparents as things to be seen only on holidays! Yet one of the first things I had noticed in adjusting to life in Honolulu was how the Asian moppets always seemed to hike to elementary school with a grandma in tow. I couldn't help envying those Asian oldies. Significance? The time had come to divest ourselves of the glib explanations we were eager to foist on our visitors, and learn to listen to what was really on their minds.

Not long afterward I had a second epiphany. In those days I hosted a weekly radio program, "Pacific Profile," in which I pumped an unending line of interesting visitors for tidbits of their expertise. Today's visitor had been a puzzle, the editor of the leading paper in the Indian state of Kerala, which was then the center of Communist ideology in that subcontinent. By the time the interview was over I felt thoroughly battered by the man's ideological body-blows, and seeking a peaceful common ground during our drive to the airport, I started to talk about Thomas Jefferson.

"Ah, Jefferson, that slave-holding partisan of freedom," he began, as I swerved to miss an errant lane-cutter on the freeway. But he then shifted abruptly to his favorite Tom story. "Did you know that Jefferson almost got arrested in Italy for secreting a new and embargoed variety of rice in a hollow cane?"

No, I replied, that was news to me.

Now I consider myself something of a Jefferson buff. I had read "Notes on Virginia" and knew all about how Jefferson was researching new possibilities for agriculture in his home state as he traveled around Europe. Why had I missed this tasty item? It was simple. I was not from a Third World country, where an impending agricultural revolution was turning out to be the difference between life and death to starving millions.

Patrick D. Hazard
Weimar, Germany

# 23 Nick

One of the best students I ever had was a Minneapolis kid named Nick Gadbois. After a few days of various procedures and demonstrations of techniques I asked the students to draw large, on good paper and in ink. Ink cannot be smudged like charcoal nor erased like pencil. Ink drawing demands preparation and decision, I believed. The students were required to keep portfolios of their work, which they would then tack or tape to the wall for critiques. We didn't call the portfolios "sketchbooks" for I reminded them very often that a drawing was a visual *idea*, and a sketch was just a passing thought at best. We want drawing, I told them, not sketchy baloney.

On the days appointed for critiques the drawings would appear on the wall. There they were, large, clean, lovely, powerful and in ink, sometimes with wash. But wait! In the middle of these were tiny drawings in pencil by my friend Nick. (He also did big ones in ink.) The other students tried to dump on Nick's pencil drawings, expecting me to concur. But how could anybody say anything negative about these exquisite little professional drawings? They were gems, all of them. One in particular was astonishing. It was in the renaissance triangular composition mode—classical conception—on a square piece of fine paper no more than eight inches high. Andy Warhol was sitting on a chair. Looking cool, impassive even bland, with a glint of light reflected off his dark sunglasses, he was surrounded by a roomful of opulent baroque gear. It was a very funny play of contrasts. I think only Nick and I knew how good and how funny it was.

Some months later Andy Warhol himself came to the Coffman Union for a showing of his latest films. His friends were with him, among them Viva and Joe Delasandro. There was only a small audience because the films were mostly immensely dull. "Empire," for example, was an eight-hour view through a stationary camera of the Empire State Building. Moreover, it was rumored that Andy Warhol had sent an impersonator of himself, that he was shy and reclusive and, today, absent. He was widely known to have done this in the past.

But I'd met the real Andy Warhol some years before and he was here, clad in blue jeans and a leather jacket. One of the graduate students, Mary Sine, kept asking him, as if he were an impostor, what the real Andy Warhol would have thought of this and that, how did Andy come by his ideas, and what was Andy's attitude toward—whatever it was. Andy kept answering dutifully what he thought Andy thought about this and that. I was finding it difficult to control my laughter. Andy caught on to this and winked at me, then continued his reverse masquerade, enjoying it every bit as much as I did.

Then I remembered Nick's drawing. So I crossed the river to the Art building, found Nick, and suggested that he show the drawing to Andy—that he was the real thing. We went back together. Even though the conversation was low-key and friendly, Nick was as shy as Andy. Finally he said that he had a drawing that he'd like to show him.

"Let's see it, kid," said Andy. "That's really a good drawing, kid," he said. "I like it a lot. Can I have it?"

"Sure," said Nick, tearing it out of the drawing book. "Will you do a drawing for me?"

"I'd be glad to," said Andy. Then he grabbed Nick's drawing book and produced an excellent drawing of a Campbell's soup can, wrote a warm dedication to Nick and signed it. We were all delighted. It boosted my already high estimations of both Andy Warhol and Nick Gadbois.

Is this the end of the story? Not quite. Somehow, news of this exchange leaked out to Gordon Locksley, then the darling of the hairdressing crowd. He lived in a venerable mansion on Mount Curve Avenue in Minneapolis and was famous for, among other things, his lavish parties and his excellent collection of contemporary art. That night he called Nick and offered him a huge sum of money for the drawing, sight unseen. I am happy to report that Nick refused.

Tom Egerman
Minneapolis, Minnesota

## 24 Making Love

Viewing Romeo and Juliet with my class. One way of watching those lovers is to say they are making a house with their bodies...roof, walls, windows, floor. Paintings on the wall, furniture, silverware in the pantry, music purling somewhere, pottery, a courtyard, sunlight. They are "playing house..."

When we were children we would say "playing school" in the same voice. But right now, LaKeisha watches them, putting out her hand in disbelief as they die... Bobby stops talking at last, and we are bathed in an extraordinary silence... DaJuan, who daily refuses to read a part, probes his copy of the play...

One a day like this, when there is no bad news from overnight, when no one comes in angry because a parent yelled this morning or because Corey forgot the money he owes, when no one is too hungry or sleepy or jealous; and when, for whatever reason, the day's lesson has connected with their lives, then something like love happens...We play house...and for a while we abide in that space reminding us all of the watery time we spent inside our mothers.

George Roberts
Minneapolis, Minnesota

# 25 It's a Good Thing

I was teaching Raymond Carver's "A Small Good Thing" for the first time to a sophomore level short story class. The story had deeply touched me. Perhaps the fact that we were nearing the end of a difficult semester made me especially vulnerable to the tenderness of the baker who earlier in the story had been called a "bastard" and an "evil son of a bitch" by the grieving mother. Late in the story, and late at night, the parents of the boy who has recently died show up at the bakery to castigate the baker for his innocent, yet painful, insensitivity to the parents on the phone. The scene at the bakery is a masterpiece of reconciliation, so much so that there are suggestions of communion in the sharing of the bread between the baker and the parents. The bread is "heavy…but rich," and tastes of "molasses and coarse grains" …like life.

I was excited to teach this new story, but without past experience to anticipate student responses. It was late spring, a few days before the end of classes. Most of the students had the look of late spring: "Don't expect much out of me, Mr. Carlson."

We got off to a slow start. After a few mumbled responses to my questions I decided to call on Kyle, who, like the other students that sunny morning, didn't appear eager to contribute to the sputtering discussion, but who, unlike the other students, I could be quite confident had read the story and would have something to say about it. I threw him a softball: "What did you think of the story, Kyle?"

Kyle slid down in his desk. His face reddened. At the time Kyle was student body president, had participated in sports, drama and music in high school, and was an honor student. He was used to performing. His face nodded down a bit, making it impossible to have eye contact. I began to wonder how I was going to get through the remaining forty minutes. He then quietly said: "1 didn't like the story." Good grief, I thought. What now?

"Why not, Kyle?"

"Because I don't like stories that make me cry ."

John Carlson
Forest City, Iowa

# 26 Shorts and Ties

When I first started teaching high school, I wanted what every new teacher wants—to be my student's friend. Be their buddy, be close, laugh and play with them, enjoy a kind of camaraderie that movies tell about. But I was a failure at the buddy stuff. I set standards which I didn't enforce. Didn't know how. By January the classes were out of control and I was fast becoming the dictator that I hated when I was a student—the kind of teacher I vowed I'd never be, threatening, yelling, keeping kids after school. I didn't know any better then, but I learned.

The thing about threatening and intimidating and shaming students is that it destroys the playfulness, the joyful spirit that makes learning the pleasure it's meant to be. Now years and years after that bad experience, I can enjoy the playfulness my students wish to express. It spills out of their unfettered spirits and we all laugh.

Like the last day of my college honors class this year. We had worked hard on the freshman research project together. The students had produced a film instead of the standard research paper. They called it Hotel Purgatory, with rooms in the hotel representing the minds of the characters from our year's reading—Oedipus, Medea, Kurtz, Falstaff—characters who assessed their lives in flashbacks, songs, speeches.

The students did a good job, held a premiere showing for the school, and as my father would say, they were feeling "devilish." Three of the men were late for class the next day and when they walked in, they were wearing only boxer shorts and neckties.

What's a teacher to do? Well, first we all laughed. Then I welcomed the "naked contingent" and our discussion began.

My opening questions was, "What conception of justice do you have now that has changed from the notion you held at the beginning of this course?" One of the

women started; she was serious, talking about individuals who determine justice. One of my "naked contingent," Mr. Z. talked about justice with a big "J," an objective meaning of justice that each person is called to, but may show itself in a "clouded" way.

I watched Mr. Z. as he talked, engaged with his subject, articulate, sure of himself, yet "naked" in his Minnesota white skin, nineteen-year-old not-quite-developed body, Valentine shorts, no doubt his graduation tie, and I thought, "You must not laugh." But then I caught the eye of a woman across the circle from me, her face red, her cheeks puffed with stifled laughter and we both burst out with hard belly laughs. The whole class joined us. Mr. Z. looked startled, amazed, but being a good sport, he too chuckled.

And then a curious thing happened: the discussion changed its focus and we began to talk about the responsibilities in forming a covenant, the justice involved, and one asked, "Can a society that invites you to join by giving up some of your liberties in order to protect your life then in turn take your life?" We argued about conscription and pacifism; one student's father had been in Vietnam, one's grandfather in World War II. Shorts-and-ties-only were ignored as everyone argued hard and well.

When class was over, one student said as he left: "Well, we sure went out with a bang, didn't we! That was the best discussion we had all year." It wasn't the discussion I had planned: we hadn't pulled all we had learned together, we hadn't probed for new insights that our readings may have inspired, we didn't reassess, analyze or synthesize as I had hoped. Instead I watched the three pull their pants out of their bookbags, facing the corner as they zipped up, and I heard one of them say, "We should have asked the women. Maybe they would have come in their underwear too."

Elizabeth Stoltz
North St. Paul, Minnesota

# 27  Creative Discussion

As I look back on my teaching career, I remember with wry amusement a seminar I taught on the Art of the Memoir at Macalaster College. I had a teaching preceptor —only the second time in my twenty-odd years of teaching—who got credit for being a kind of assistant teacher. He was a senior, filled with idealism. One seminar, when we were about to discuss Peter Mathiessen's *The Snow Leopard,* my assistant—let's call him George—asked me if he couldn't lead the class in the first part of our two-hour session. I agreed, and sat back while he elicited lively discussion about Buddhism, drug use, hallucinations, mysticism, the meaning of life—and lots more.

After a short break, I took over. "Okay, so what did you actually think about this book?" I asked. "Did you like it?" Silence. I went around the class. "Martha, did YOU like this book?" "Well, actually, I haven't finished it yet," Martha said. "Tom?" Tom said he wasn't very far into it. How far? The first chapter? No? The first page? Ah, the book jacket.

So it went, all around the circle. Only one member of the class had actually finished the reading. I smiled, a little grimly, and turned to George, my assistant. "You see how verbally gifted this group is?" I inquired. "You have just led a vigorous discussion on a book almost none of them has actually read."

I brooded a little out loud. "Too bad," I said. "I was about to ask you to compare this to Mary McCarthy's memoir from last week, but. .." I was interrupted. "Yes, Tom?"

Not at all deflated, Tom began, "I think I see a real difference in style when…" I interrupted him. "Tom," I asked incredulously, "are you about to tell me you think you can compare the style of two books, one of which you haven't read?" Tom nodded, but I stopped him again. "No," I said firmly. "I admire your creativity, but I have my own limitations. I really don't want to hear any more until you've read the book. And now I think we'll all go home. "

Next week everyone had done the reading. Or at least, I think they had.

Susan Toth
St. Paul, Minnesota

# 28 Water Marks

A s I write these words, I haven't got a chair or a table, but I'm surrounded by piles of books, heaped on the floor.

During the flood, now called, like a generalissimo, the Great Spring Flood of 1997, our house in Grand Forks shipped six to seven feet of water on the main floor. Because our property lay close to the river, the emergency dike had been built up into the front yard. When the river finally overwhelmed the city, the peculiar effect of the dike was to hold water inside the house for three weeks while the river slowly receded. When we were permitted to return, longtime teachers and writers that we are, my husband and I first tried to salvage our hundreds of books. We failed utterly, despite our best efforts using baby powder, wax paper, and toothbrushes, and the too small freezing compartment of our refrigerator.

Well beyond repair, the house has since been cleaned out and gutted. In the process, we discovered that our insulation consisted of packets of 1939 newspapers, now moldy and sodden. Every once in a awhile the workers would stop ripping them out long enough to read the wedding and war news. Through all our years in the house, words had housed us; we had been insulated by the written histories of lives in the walls around us.

I've forgotten the name of the poet in Chaucer's time who wrote everything out in Latin, French, and English, praying that one of those languages would survive to keep him immortal. (He's been reduced to an anecdote.) We realized, of course, that it's lunatic to live by, and in, words, which evaporate as soon as they are breathed out, or by sheets of paper; we can't ever save them. They return to earth, air, water, fire: their elements.

Now the passionate conspiracy of friends has brought several big boxes to our apartment door; in them, inscribed copies of books from dozens and dozens of writers wishing us milder weather and good reading. If we don't know another way to live, if we insist on sailing an ark made of paper keeping our names and loves alive, we can all work the impossible together. Beyond any doubt, my husband and I know ourselves to be part of a glorious, go-for-broke company everywhere. Water covers paper, but paper covers rock. Teachers, writers, readers, students: books possess us all.

Martha Meek
Minneapolis, Minnesota

# 29  Learning About Suicide

Every day in Room 101, my third grade classroom, there are many things for the children and teacher to learn about, including the suicide of Willie's father.

Willie was a child from a single parent family. His mother had told me that the divorce had been a bitter one. One Thursday afternoon the principal came to my door and asked me to step out into the hallway, where he informed me that Willie's father had gone to his wife's place of employment and shot himself dead in front of her and her co-workers. "Willie is to be told that his mother called," said the principal, "and he should go to his grandmother's house after school." The principal also asked me to be at school at 7:30 on Monday morning for a meeting with social workers and grief counselors. "They will help you deal with this in your class," he said. "Willie will be back in school on Monday." Returning to the class room, I gave Willie the message, and soon the dismissal bell rang.

I met the following Monday morning with the grief counselors and social workers, who were all very helpful. They showed much insight and perceptiveness in answering my questions. I assumed they would accompany me to class and help me deal with my third graders, including Willie, but when the meeting broke up they wished me luck and began to leave. "Will I be able to do this by myself?" I asked. "Shouldn't you be there too?"

"No," one of them said, "you need to go to your class alone. You are their security, you are the one who needs to help them through this process."

I went to my classroom, greeted my students and said, "I'm sure you are all aware that Willie's father died over the weekend. I want Willie to know how sorry we all are about this."

One student's hand went up immediately. He said, "Willie, why did your dad kill himself?"

Silence.

I said that we might not ever know what happened, that perhaps he was very sad about something, and he had great difficulty dealing with his sadness. I said that no one, not even Willie, would ever be able to answer that question adequately.

Another student spoke up. He described, eloquently, what it is like to lose someone you love. "My grandfather died last year, and I loved him a lot." he said. "When somebody like that dies, it's like getting a cut. At first, you bleed a lot and you are in much pain. Gradually the bleeding stops and the pain gets better. Pretty soon a scar forms. That scar stays for a long time to remind you of the pain you had. The scar never goes away, although it becomes more and more faint as time goes on."

I went on to say that what we needed to do was to continue to be a classroom working together, helping one another, doing our assignments, and providing the same routine for Willie that he was used to. "We are all here for Willie, any way he needs us," I said, and we went about our day, closer than ever before.

Mary Payton
Waunakee, Wisconsin

# 30 Like a Sacrament

I have always loved teaching—loved the preparation and classroom dialogue, loved the way students' insights and questions stimulated my thinking and sometimes subverted and reshaped my approach, loved the time for reading and the conversations among colleagues. But there were some academic practices which I abhorred, especially correcting papers and assigning grades. And there were onerous expectations of the institution under the rubric of "faculty services"—a phrase I had often thought of as merely a euphemism for bondage to the endless series of committee, departmental and faculty meetings which interrupted the real stuff of education.

Then one day I happened upon an essay by Simone Weil. "Every school exercise," she wrote, "is like a sacrament." Exercise? Really? How much grading had she had to do, I wondered? How many meetings cluttered her calendar? But Weil's words wouldn't let go of me. Could I make it so?

A funny thing happened on the way to my next committee meeting. I tried to imagine what a "sacramental meeting" might look like. Could we gather for "holy conversation" around matters of schedule and budget, in-service planning and grant requests, faculty evaluations and hiring decisions? I tried to think what might characterize our exchange. There would be a sense of presence, an encounter of persons, a careful listening and response, a generous acceptance of mission. Thinking thus can make it so. It's often simply a matter of perspective. Meetings, I have gradually come to recognize, provide an opportunity for collegial *administration*—literally *ministry* or *service* exercised in communion with one another. Meetings are a ritual of stewardship and an exercise of trust. Does such reflection make meetings less onerous, easier to attend? Most of the time. Not always. But it does give me a different attitude.

And what about grading? How does one grade "sacramentally"? Reading papers and assigning grades can be so time-consuming. The task is burdensome, especially for large classes and long essays. Then I had the insight: what better way to spend my time than in this exchange of gifts. Grading is an act of justice and an act of truth-telling. It is also an act of love. I do think of it now as gift-giving. My students make a gift of their insights and observations to me. At the same time they reveal themselves in what they write. Can I do less than reciprocate? Grading has become a way for me to acknowledge the gift, to comment on its uniqueness, to recognize its usefulness, to write an appropriate response.

On the surface of things—before and after Weil—my academic life is unchanged. But the way I think about the academic vocation with its numerous "school exercises" has been transformed by her wisdom.

Kathleen Hughes, RSCJ
St. Louis, Missouri

# 31 Out to Lunch

The quarter was barely a few weeks old, but already a pattern had emerged. Class would begin at 6:00 PM or shortly thereafter. Patrick would arrive at 6:45—or shortly thereafter. It all happened as if by clockwork. It wasn't a noisy, splashy entrance. It wasn't even a disruptive entrance. But it was noticed. Patrick would saunter in without the slightest hint of embarrassment, and once inside the room he would head straight for the same empty seat. The empty seat right in front of me. No matter that this classroom had plenty of empty seats from which to choose. The routine was, to put it mildly, more than mildly unsettling. Patrick, you see, was young and black. I, need it be said, am neither.

What made matters more unsettling was Patrick's pose once he had settled in. Note-taking was not on his short list of things to do. Arms folded, legs stretched in front of him, Patrick was in full slouch. He was not soon asleep— or heading anywhere toward sleep. No matter the topic, no matter what he hadn't heard me say on the topic, Patrick had a question—and a comment. Or was it the other way around? Generally, his opinion was informed or at least semi-informed. And the outspokenness? He was there to learn, he said. I believed him. But I also reminded him that learning and silence were not necessarily mutually exclusive enterprises. More than that, I reminded him that others were there to learn as well. All pretty conventional stuff. How did Patrick take it? Hard to say.

More often than not, Patrick's comments were worth hearing, even if they were designed to show off. Often they were provocative. Inevitably they were disruptive, certainly more so than his entrance. But that didn't bother

Patrick. Whether his running commentary interrupted the logic—or at least the flow—of the lecture mattered not a whit to him. It was as though there was no lecture being delivered at all. Indeed, to Patrick it was as though he and I were the only two people in the room. This was not only unsettling to me, but it was also unsettling to those few dozen people in the room with us. The looks on their faces told me that they were already in full consumer mode, as in "I didn't pay tuition to listen to someone other than the teacher carry on."

Something had to be done. I chose break time of week three to have a little chat with Patrick. The lateness? It seems that he had just started a new job at the local bank. It ended at 5:30, but since he was without a car and reliant on the bus for transportation, he was doing his best to arrive when he did. And oh, by the way, his job had been found for him by the president of my college. Patrick was also the vice-president of the student senate. And the outspokenness? He was there to learn, he said. I believed him.

Week Four. Patrick arrived on Patrick time—6:45 or thereabouts. But this time he arrived armed. Loaded down with a Burger King bag, he searched for the seat that he had assigned himself. It was vacant. This time Patrick did not fold his arms and stick out his legs. No, this time Patrick was fully upright and engaged. Out came the contents of the bag. In short order, he had spread before himself a three course Burger King bonanza of hamburger, fries and a malt.

As he went about his business (of preparing to eat), I went about my business (of pretending to lecture). The topic at the moment escapes me. Whatever it was, the possibility that I was making any sense of it was, at best, doubtful. That's because I wasn't thinking about what I was saying or about to say next. Instead I was thinking about what Patrick was doing—and about to do next. And a week following our little chat, no less!

In the midst of trying to keep my composure—and of momentarily pretending to ignore what could not be ignored—my thoughts on the historical topic at hand took a distant back seat to my thoughts about the loaded moment at hand. If this was a white kid, I'd be all over him, was the thought that crystallized everything. As soon as I said that to myself (who knows what I was saying out loud to my students) I knew what followed logically—and what I would have to say immediately.

What followed logically was this: to ignore Patrick was engaging in a not so subtle form of racism. After all, what is racism but treating people differently because of the color of their skin? To "get all over a white kid" and let a black kid eat his dinner (and have me for lunch at the same time) was to be, let's be honest, a racist. The only solution was "get all over the black kid." Which I proceeded to do.

"Patrick, what are you doing?"

"I'm eating."

"Why?"

"I'm hungry."

"Patrick, if you're hungry and want to eat, go down to the cafeteria."

"But I want to learn."

"Then put the food away."

Which he did without comment or complaint. And that was the end of that. Was I stunned that I had said anything at all? Not really. My faulty tendency, no matter how uncomfortable the classroom situation, is to say nothing for far too long and then say a mouthful all at once. Was the rest of the class stunned that I said something? Not really. I learned later that many were just waiting for the inevitable set-to. Was I stunned that Patrick complied? Not really. Was it all a test of sorts? Probably. Our chat of the week before had revealed an engaging kid who really did want to learn. An angry kid he wasn't. An ambitious kid he was. When I had suggested that he cut back on student politics and concentrate on his studies and his bank job, his reply was revealing as well. He couldn't do that; politics, after all, was his "ticket" to making something of himself.

Has he done that? To date, I simply don't know. Patrick did pass my course, and respectably so. And he did it a) without ever showing up on time; b) without ever again appearing with his dinner; c) without ever not finding the chair right in front of me; and d) with a greater willingness to keep his opinions, but not his questions, to himself. The larger and more important question of whether Patrick has had his success ticket punched remains unanswered, at least by me.

Chuck Chalberg
Bloomington, Minnesota

# 32  Found Poems

I recorded curious sentences students wrote. With two exceptions, all the sentences included here were written in my classroom: weekly journals, vocabulary sentences, and essays.

I converted some student writing into *Found Poems*, following simple rules: maintain student spelling and punctuation, avoid juxtaposition of sentences, neither delete nor add words. I did, obviously, line their sentences, making poems.

Stan Smith
Minder, Nebraska

I do not like to read.
I can not read good.
I can not spell.
My borther can not read.
I dream that I can read.

School is perty fun.
School helps you learn things
like how to reed and write and add
and stuff like that.
I just might end up in collgee
I hop so.
like my borther.

We have a game Thursday.
My brother law is coming down to watch me.
That makes me fell good inside
because my brother law likes football
the sport of contack.
I want to kill em.
I want to make handburger out of em.

Yesterday was a very bad day.
Ricky got killed.
I couldn't believe it.
I saw him Friday.
Later I went hunting.

A pheasant flew up.
I got him on the first shot.
I stepped on its head and pulled the legs up.
Its head came off.
The bird kind of cheered me up.
But it didn't bring Ricky back.
I got up.
I ate brakefast.
I watched cartoon.
Me and my brother killed a cat.

I am looking for a girl that likes kids.
That don't look too bad.
That is not to much older than me.
I would like to live down on the river like my dad
and fram the side hills and get some catle
and some pig and some hourse and maybe
she wont even like to live out there.

# 33 Mud Time

I recall a gray April afternoon in 1968, sitting in
American Literature class, listening to Mrs. Shaffer,
my eleventh grade college-prep English teacher, read to

the class Roberts Frost's "Two Tramps in Mud Time."
We followed along in our book as she came to the last
stanza:

> *But yield who will to their separation,*
> *My object in living is to unite*
> *My avocation and my vocation*
> *As my two eyes make one in sight.*
> *Only where love and need are one,*
> *And the work is play for mortal stakes,*
> *Is the deed ever really done*
> *For Heaven and the future's sakes.*

When she finished, I recall being somewhat confused by the
last stanza—what exactly was "the work is play for mortal
stakes"? When she asked for questions or comments, I
raised my hand. I remember the class wrestling with
the poem's meaning, as we did with most of the poems
we studied that spring in Mrs. Shaffer's unit on modern
poetry. And like most of Mrs. Shaffer's class discussions
on modern poetry, it was a lively and spirited match. I
don't recall that we came to any definite conclusions about
the poem that afternoon, but I do know that when I left
her classroom I knew I was alive, and that my love for
literature and poetry was a right love.

Mrs. Shaffer was among the few teachers who, early
on, acknowledged my love for literature and poetry and

nourished it in me. Now, I don't recall that she ever praised me publicly or took me aside and said "Son, you're a brilliant student of literature, and what you're doing is right. I support your decision to be an English major in college." No, I think it was something much more subtle, something more elusive, beyond the grasp of words. And she certainly would have been wrong about the "brilliant" part, if she had ever said that. Perhaps it was the gentle way she managed to tell me that Hemingway is spelled with one "m" not two. Perhaps it was the way she asked if she could read my poems sometime.

Perhaps it was our many conversations about literature and art (she was also a fine painter) both in and out of class. I don't know. But somehow she knew I was serious about literature and poetry, and she was not going to let anything undermine my seriousness. I think the tone of her voice, her demeanor, her countenance—even more so than her words—said "I know you're serious about this stuff. I know how you feel. I feel the same way. I respect that. Even though you're a muddle-headed sixteen-year-old boy who has absolutely no idea what the world is about and what it holds in store for you, I know this stuff means something to you and I honor that. I'll help as much as I can, but you'll have to figure it out yourself." How much of the power and influence of teachers is beyond the subject matter they teach us and the words they speak to us?

Two years later, away at college and lugging around my beefy and battered copies of the Norton anthologies of literature, because I was now an English major, I received a letter from my mother-along with a clipping torn from my home town newspaper—telling me that Mrs. Shaffer was dead. Although the circumstances surrounding her death were reported, the cause of death was never stated directly. To me—and I think to anyone else reading that clipping—it was obvious that her death was a suicide.

Stunned, I thought about how young she was at the time of her death—not quite forty. I thought it impossible that anyone so young and so vital could find no more reasons—not even one—to live. I remember thinking that maybe if Mrs. Shaffer and I could have had one of our discussions about literature, and I could have told her how right she was about the way she treated me and my growing adolescent infatuation with literature and poetry a few years ago, she would have had at least one reason to live. If she did it for me, then she needed to be there for others like me because we need people like her to be there for us. I remember walking down to the campus lake that day and weeping, and then later that evening trying to write something in my notebook about her death. I'd like to say I wrote something profound or insightful, but I have no record or recollection of what I wrote that evening.

The semester after her death, when I was wrestling with my own decisions about work and my commitment to writing, once again I found myself reading Frost in my college course on modem poetry. It was then, I think, that I finally came to understand what Frost is talking about in that last stanza—and what I had wrestled with in Mrs. Shaffer's eleventh grade English class a few years earlier. Of course, "Two Tramps in Mud Time" is a poem about the proper relationship to work. The speaker in the poem suspects that the two tramps who come along while he is chopping wood might be after his job. I believe the last stanza resolves the speaker's dilemma about his relationship to work: "My object in living is to unite / My avocation and my vocation." That has guided me and my relationship with my work and commitment to literature and poetry ever since.

Years later, I did write a poem about Mrs. Shaffer. I doubt that it explains anything actual about her life and death. Truth is muddier than what we are usually capable of describing. I suspect the poem is more about my groping for understanding than it is about the mystery or facts of her death.

### Sarah Shaffer

*Your canvases gave no indication,*
*nor did the lectures on the modern poem.*
*But that morning when you came downstairs to*

*where the car sat, each step down became a*
*careful conjugation of what your life*
*had been all about. Settling yourself*
*in the seat, your tired hand found the key*
*as you waited for asphyxiation.*

*And when they found you, someone quickly came*
*to clarify the ambiguities*
*and dispel any thought of suicide,*
*though somehow "accident" could not explain*
*you below the house, perfectly defined,*
*in the quiet oxide of exhaustion.*

Perhaps revelation comes only when we are ready and capable of understanding it; or maybe revelation comes, like grace, when we least expect it; or maybe it never comes at all. Those among us who have been blessed with such teachers are well aware of their power. We need time to tramp around in mud. And we need teachers who will grant us our time there and not force us through it or out of it sooner than we need to be. Sarah Shaffer stood on the other side of the mud pond urging me on, allowing me my time in the mud.

Thom Tammaro
Moorhead, Minnesota

# Failing

I am last to leave the office suite on a November afternoon, and I see him approach in the twilit hallway. I know him first by his shambling walk and, as he draws closer, by the way his eyes shine with a moist and needy kind of brightness. His name is Bruce. At his side is a girl carrying a baby and a bulging diaper bag. Bruce has taken three of my classes over the past six years. I last saw him a year or so ago when I wished him luck as he set out for Montana to mine silver. The year before that I wished him luck as he set out for New Jersey to work for Standard Oil.

"Bruce, how's it going?" I ask, shaking his hand.

"Really well," he tells me, "really well. I'm up north cutting pulp."

The baby begins to cry, and I notice that it's astonishingly new, not more than two weeks old.

"Who are your friends?" I have to ask him, for he's staring at me with a trancelike smile on his handsome face.

"Oh yeah, this is Angie and Timmy."

Angie, a pretty, waiflike girl who can't be more than seventeen, moves off toward a restroom with the baby.

"Are you considering school again?" I ask him. Bruce has enrolled on this campus at least three times without completing a semester. One time he was my best student, twice he was my worst. Erratic scholarship always makes me suspect drug use or insanity. In Bruce's case, I'd assumed it was drugs because of a remark he made in class a couple of years ago. It was the day he came to class with the left side of his face, chin to hairline, plastered with gauze and tape, and I asked him what happened. "I don't know," he said with a shrug and a guilty smile. "I wasn't there at the time."

"Yeah, I'm thinking about getting back into reading," he tells me. "See, we live in this cabin a long ways from anyplace and it's great for reading books, but my reading is all hit-and-miss, you know? So what I figure I'll do, I'll come back and get my degree in literature and then I'll know what to read."

"And what will you do for a living, teach?"

"No, no, I'll keep cutting down trees. See, I've finally got my future figured out—I want to be the only pulp-cutter in Minnesota with a B.A." He gives me an expanded smile that seems to intensify the drug-induced brightness of his eyes. I've never known anyone else's eyes to shine like Bruce's. They pierce me with steadiness, and I have to look away.

"It's wonderful what you can get out of books," he continues. "There's a book teaches you how to deliver babies, you know? I read it and delivered Timmy up at our cabin." Wanting to see my reaction to this, he steps around so that he can bore into me again with his eyes. He obviously wants to know what I think of this.

I'm aghast, imagining the pain and exertion and false moves in that remote cabin in the north woods as Bruce and Angie struggle to do what doctors accomplish only after years of preparation.

"It's a thrill," he prompts. "It' really a thrill to bring a new life into the world."

"Yes, certainly," I manage to say. "It must have been thrilling." This baby is Bruce's second child. He was married to someone else when I first knew him, a portly woman who looked much older than Bruce, and who moved far away and took their little daughter with her. I am overcome with a sense of foreboding. I foresee tough times for his wife and son as they careen along the reckless course of life Bruce will lead them on. My dire premonition expands to include everyone victimized by the self-serving of this world who seem to be proliferating like rabbits. Surely this will lead to a new Dark Age.

Angie emerges from the rest room, saying, "Hush

now, hush now," and trying to appease the baby with a pacifier.

Bruce frowns in their direction and murmurs, "You need peace and quiet to read."

We part company then, Angie smiling sadly, Bruce assuring me once more how well things are going, now that he's coming to grips with his future. "Really *really* well," he says.

The next day, in the faculty lounge, I learn that Bruce came to town to file for divorce, and he passed through campus on his way to Angie's home town, where he will deposit her—his bride of six months— and Timmy—his son of less than a month—with her parents.

You need peace and quiet to read.

Jon Hassler

# 34 Joshua

Joshua wore his curly hair long so it framed his narrow face. Mondays through Thursdays he dressed in faded polo shirts and ragged bell-bottoms with sandals. On Friday he had a mesh pullover which showed the sparse hair around his nipples. It was orange. He was cool. I didn't like him.

He began in the middle of the room. I soon brought him down front. Later, when I'd exhausted my arsenal of threats and cajolery, he went to the back where he slept peacefully until Shelley.

Percy Bysshe Shelley, who wrote the poem "Ozymandias" in 1817, entered Joshua's life when I asked the class to memorize the poem and they moaned their displeasure and he was awakened.

Without raising her hand, Marta Tomas said, "Memorization as an educational tool is outdated and ineffectual. And it sucks. That's what Mrs. Cadavid told us."

"I'm not Mrs. Cadavid."

It was Thursday and I explained how they had the whole weekend to memorize fourteen lines and even a tenth-grader could do that. We read the poem aloud together. Joshua went back to sleep.

Joshua was never rebellious, but rumor had it he was high much of the time—pot, red devils, even LSD. There was no doubt his eyes were pretty-much glazed over, I'd seen it often enough when they were open, but then Shelley and Tom Gray and even Shakespeare himself glazed more eyes than they opened and I couldn't really fault Joshua for that. It was really his attitude, that great subjective grading tool, which bugged me.

Quietly, he despised classrooms and English Literature and the writing of papers and quizzes and final exams and grades and teacher too. When I saw Joshua sleeping contentedly through my lesson plans and lectures I saw failure—not his so much as mine. Joshua was a great weight of depression that I carried through fourth period into lunch where it was multiplied by twenty minutes of lounge griping.

On Friday morning early, Mrs. Cadavid spoke to me sharply about memorization as an educational tool. As passé as the brassiere she said, and went off bouncing and sagging along the hall. I began the day red-faced and grumpy. I had five preps on Fridays.

By fourth period my grumpiness had turned to stubbornness, which got me through more days of teaching than I care to remember. Joshua already had his head down on his folded arms by the time I'd taken roll and answered the list of questions I'd answered the day before: Do we have to write it or just say it? If we write it do we have to spell the words right? What's a "visage" and how can a heart be fed?

"So," I said. "Who has it memorized?"

"You just assigned it yesterday," Marta Tomas reminded me. "That's unfair."

Joshua raised his hand. Something he'd never done.

I called his name and he stood beside his desk and I thought him rather an imposing figure there at the back of the room silhouetted against the white concrete wall. His hands were quiet and folded in front of him.

Joshua tilted back his head of dark red curls and recited "Ozymandias" with the panache of Richard Burton, and when he finished the classroom was stilled.

It's been twenty-seven years since Joshua recited that poem for me and I still don't know why he did it, but after he did it we were never the same with each other. He greeted me at the classroom door and I greeted him. We smiled a kind of knowing smile as if we kept a mutual secret. Joshua slept through the remainder of his senior year and never completed another assignment or bothered with tests and I flunked him. He didn't care.

Jimmy Olsen
St. Cloud, Minnesota

## 35 The International Student

In fall of 1994, I had a new student from Latvia named Olivers Wilkes. Although Tennessee Wesleyan's ESL program consisted mostly of Japanese students, *perestroika* had brought about an influx of Russian students as well, and the Latvian Olivers along with them.

I picked up Olivers at the airport in Knoxville and was dismayed to discover that he spoke practically *no* English at all. I took him to campus a few days before fall semester. As Spanish is my second language and I speak *very* little Russian, let alone Latvian (which is somewhat similar to Russian), I tried to explain to him that orientation would begin on the following Monday morning. I took him to get bed linens and snack foods, showed him the cafeteria, and dropped him off at the dormitory, assuming that with his linguistic barrier he'd just stay in the dorm until Monday. He kept saying "car" and "I have international drive card." I kept saying, "Well, how nice." I should have paid more attention.

I had just started dating a young lady whom I had invited over for dinner on the Saturday evening before the beginning of orientation on Monday. She was scheduled to arrive at 7:00, and at 6:10 I was busy cooking. The phone rang, so I propped it on my shoulder and continued cooking. What I heard forced me to turn off the burner on the stove and sit down.

"Is this Mr. Yankee?"

"Who?"

"Mr. Yankee? Or, do you have a student named Olivers Wilkes?"

"Yes."

"Well, I'm an international operator with AT&T. Mr. Wilkes is stranded in Knoxville and needs your help."

"That's impossible! I took him to campus just the other day. He only arrived in the country a few days ago."

As Tennessee Wesleyan is in Athens, Tennessee, a one-hour drive from Knoxville, I felt that what the operator was telling me was highly unlikely. However, the fact that he had the student's name and a fair approximation of mine by international standards gave me a sinking feeling.

"Well, Mr. Wilkes has driven his car to Knoxville and run out of gas. He walked to a pay phone and spoke with us until they figured out he speaks Russian and put me on the phone. He wasn't sure of your name, but apparently you gave him your phone number."

A mistake I questioned making again.

"Where is Olivers?"

"Well, he's not sure, but he's downtown and parked in front of a tall, blue building."

"I'll bet that's the former United American Bank once owned by the infamous Jake Butcher."

"I don't know sir. I'm in New York."

"I do. It's the only big blue building in Knoxville. Where did he get a car?!?"

"I don't know, sir."

"What does he want me to do about this?"

"To come get him, sir."

"Thank you very much."

I called and extended my regrets to the young lady. (Oddly, we didn't see each other after that. Go figure.)

I drove the one-hour drive to Knoxville, went downtown to Gay Street and saw a Chrysler LeBaron parked half on and half off the sidewalk in front of the building. As I drove up, Olivers ran out to my car from the entry way of the building. He was obviously quite relieved and muttering something in Latvian. With his language barrier, he was unable to understand what I was saying to him, which is a good thing. By my tone, he understood that he had erred.

I had brought my gas can, so we went the two-mile distance to the nearest gas station. Of course, Olivers had no money, so I bought him a can of gas and took him back to his car. We put the gas in his car and finally got his car started. He followed me back to the same gas station, where I put a half-tank of gas into his car. He followed me back to Athens staying within ten feet of my rear bumper the entire hour's drive back, which was quite nerve-wracking.

There was one good thing about that day. One of the Russian students from the previous summer semester had returned from semester break by the time Olivers and I got back to campus. As the Russian student had become quite proficient at English, and Russian and Latvian are quite similar, he was able to translate for us.

In the one-hour drive back from Knoxville most of my anger had abated. However, I scolded Olivers soundly. It turned out his parents had given him traveler's checks for the academic year for spending money, and he'd always wanted a car. He used his international driver's license and almost *all* of his traveler's checks to purchase the used LeBaron. Apparently, used car salesmen will go to almost any lengths to make a sale. The problem was that even though Olivers spoke English well enough to buy the car, he couldn't speak it well enough to buy gasoline. What little gas was in the tank was just enough to get him to Knoxville.

Olivers lasted one year at Tennessee Wesleyan and then went back home—he couldn't pass the exit exam for the ESL program. I'd like to say I hated to see him go, but his impetuous nature also carried over into his study habits (or lack of such habits), and he was basically wasting his parent's money.

Bart Jenkins
Chattanooga, Tennessee

# 36 Sue and Tom

It was a large classroom, unremarkable except for the two eight-inch wide metal posts which emerged in the middle of the space, rising to support a massive beam in the ceiling. Someone had enlivened the posts with orange paint, but even so, after a few days of familiarity, I ceased to be aware of their presence. That is, until the first day *it* happened.

The class of sixty or more students filled the old room, with desks dodging the orange posts. I was responding to a question about Teddy Roosevelt the first time I noticed. Twenty-five feet away, a female head angled away from vertical and disappeared behind the post. Almost immediately, a male body on the opposite side of the post engaged in a similar contortion, and both heads remained out of sight for many seconds.

The orange post wasn't that wide, so I had a pretty good idea of what I had seen, but confirmation came quickly. Ten minutes later as a student on the far end asked a question, the heads disappeared again. By sliding slightly toward the questioner, I gained full vision of a long and passionate kiss. Over the next few class periods, I was treated to several more public displays of affection, including one nicely framed by a large brimmed straw hat that turned parallel to the post as its owner disappeared from view.

When the first exam came, my lovers remained united, earning matching "F's." She soon appeared in my office, tearful, asking for advice on how she could do better on the next exam. I showed her a good essay written by a classmate, and asked if she thought that her main problem was getting her ideas down in an essay or understanding the material. When she admitted that she didn't recognize much of what had appeared in the good essay, I somewhat sadistically suggested that I might be better able to help her if I could see her class notes. As I suspected, there were lots of hearts and little else. Unable to resist, I finally suggested that she might be able to learn more if she paid more attention to discussion and less to "Tom" while in class.

Without missing a beat, she asked, "What do you mean?"

"Well, it must be pretty hard to take notes when you are kissing," I replied.

At that, she let out a gasp, followed by an astonished "You saw us?" Exercising great restraint, I merely nodded yes.

For the next several class periods, both "Sue" and "Tom" were models of studiousness. Though they continued to select the desks by the orange posts, their heads stayed in a normal position. They didn't participate in discussion unless called upon, but I harbored hopes that their minds were actually focused on history. Soon, however, my illusions were shattered as temptation won. The heads stayed in place, but the hands surreptitiously glided behind the post, mingling in a less obtrusive, but no doubt distracting reminder of their mutual affection.

The short burst of attention evidently did help, for they earned dual "D's" on the second exam. Interestingly, neither came to see me for advice. Instead, a few days after

I returned the exams, two drop cards appeared pinned to my door.

As they say, love conquers all.

Ken Jones
Collegeville, Minnesota

# 37 That's What Friends Are For

Every spring, toward the end of the school year, I begin the ritual of cleaning out my classroom closet. Some years I am diligent and fill the dumpster with out-of-date books, old folders, faded construction paper scraps, and boxes of other unnecessary items that seem to reproduce in the darkness of that four by six room. Other years, I merely tidy things up and slam the door, knowing I'll regret my lackadaisical attitude come fall. And every year I come upon the same red notebook, the notebook tucked away on the bottom shelf, filled with Jenny's poetry. It has followed me from school to school, from classroom closet to classroom closet. And every year, a sadness sweeps over me...

Jenny was in eighth grade when I taught her English. She was one of those girls that you hear about in the faculty room. Stories of how needy she was. How her sixth grade teacher was relieved when she passed into junior high. Jenny had had what everyone called a schoolgirl crush on Ms. Meyers, showering her with letters and presents. But I hadn't noticed anything particularly different about Jenny. She did her work. She was in the "slow group"—back then we had three sections of every grade and they were ability grouped. She seemed plenty bright, as so many of those kids in that group were. Maybe she had been placed there because she was absent a lot. Or maybe she'd had a little trouble reading in first grade and got put in a "lower" reading group. Kids rarely moved out of one group into the next. Too much catching up to do, I guess.

Then Jenny turned in a poem, and I wrote a comment on it, encouraging her to keep writing. I can't remember what I wrote, just one of those comments teachers make—like the stars or stickers that show up in the early grades. That afternoon she stood at the classroom door after everyone else had left. I beckoned her in, wondering if she needed help diagramming a sentence or telling a subject pronoun from an object one. But no, Jenny wasn't interested in the grammar we were all working so hard at. "I write a lot, Mrs. Nesvig," she said. "Poetry, I like to write poetry." Then she smiled her crooked smile. I always wondered why her parents, who were so meticulous about their own appearance, didn't see that Jenny needed braces—her teeth were crooked with wide gaps between them. She rarely smiled, and when she did, her hand frequently went up to cover her mouth.

I can't remember much about that conversation. Just that Jenny seemed very shy, yet eager to talk about her writing. I must have encouraged her, probably telling her I'd like to see more of what she wrote. I was pleased that maybe one of my students cared about writing, which was something that always seemed to get lost in the daily grind of nouns and verbs and sentence structure.

Soon she was staying after school several times a week. She'd bring some writing or sometimes just come in to talk. Frequently she brought little gifts—a candle, a coffee mug, a key chain. Sometimes it was a souvenir from someplace she'd been. Often something she'd probably picked up at the drugstore next door. I'd tell Jenny not to buy me things, but she continued to do so.

I was beginning to be uncomfortable with her gifts and almost dread her visits. It was then I remembered what the sixth grade teacher had experienced. I asked her for advice, and she reminded me that Jenny would graduate soon and probably find a new teacher or adult to dote on. She was just one of those girls who needed that extra attention.

But it got worse. Jenny started to tell me that she couldn't sleep at night. She had terrible nightmares. One day she told me that she felt her soul leave her body during these dreams. Another time she said she'd dreamt she'd found my body covered in blood. I tried to discourage her from relaying these things to me. I tried to tell her they were just dreams. I figured she was making most of it up, anyway. It was obvious, too, that she was sharing these bizarre dreams with the girls in her class, who were often huddled around her. Jenny hadn't many friends, at least not until she started telling her stories. Then she came to school one day and told the girls that she had been accosted by a stranger late one night while walking home from the bus stop. She didn't tell me this story. I overheard her telling the group about it. This was one thing that I did need to talk to Jenny about so I asked her to stay after school.

She seemed embarrassed when I told her what I had heard. She assured me that she had told her parents, and the police had been called. Her family was taking care of it. She was okay and didn't want to go into any details. I suppose I should have called her mother. I was convinced, however, that this was another story Jenny had made up, along with her out-of-body experiences. At times, I did talk to Jenny's mother about her. It seemed as though she was on top of things, a little exasperated with the teenage years, maybe a little upset that Jenny confided so much in me, but seemed to genuinely care about her.

The school year came to an end none too soon. At graduation when Jenny presented me with her red poetry notebook, I hugged her and told her I would miss her. She also gave me a copy of the recording, "That's What Friends Are For," and I felt guilty that I really hadn't been a better friend to her.

My guilt turned to anger over the summer, though. Jenny started calling me at home. At first, though surprised, I was pleasant and asked how her summer was going. Then there started to be hang-up calls—two or three times a day—or calls where I'd pick up the phone and hear strange noises and then the click of the receiver. I knew it had to be Jenny. I felt like I was being stalked.

The phone calls stopped, though, when she started high school. I was relieved, even though midway through the year Jenny started visiting again. About once a month she'd show up after school. I put away my anger about the summer phone calls, and asked about high school, her family, her writing. I could handle once a month. Jenny told me about one of the teachers at her high school she had gotten close to. She was a counselor, and I was relieved to know that she was talking to someone who could probably handle her attention and strange stories better than I. I worried when Jenny showed me the scars on her arms she had inflicted with an eraser, but she promised she had stopped doing that. The counselor had helped her to stop. That seemed to be the pattern now with Jenny's stories. She would tell me something awful, but then tell me it was all fixed.

Toward the end of her high school years, Jenny stopped coming around. Her visits had grown less and less frequent, sort of dwindled down to nothing. It was a surprise, then, when several years after she would have finished high school, I received a letter with her familiar handwriting on the envelope. I opened it and began to read. Jenny was working full time now. She had tried a junior college, but had dropped out. She hoped to go back some day, but for now she was getting by living on her own. Then she wrote that she was doing really well now. She had finally gotten into therapy, and was able to face the problems of the past. I turned to the next page. Jenny wrote, "My father started sexually abusing me when I was in junior high. I never told anyone. I think, in a way, I never told myself." My face burned. My hand shook as I finished the letter. She went on to thank me for being there for her when she was younger. She wondered if maybe we couldn't get together sometime, now that she was an adult. I set the letter aside, promising myself that I'd call her in the next few days.

And I did mean to call her, but it was just a few days later that my husband asked me if I had taught a girl named Jennifer Connor. I nodded, and he passed me the newspaper he was reading. There was a picture of Jenny. It must have been her high school graduation picture. And there was the headline: "Young Woman Commits Suicide."

I never got to answer Jenny's letter. I never had lunch with her as I planned. I only have a letter, a record, and a red notebook filled with poetry.

Sandy Nesvig
St. Paul, Minnesota

# 38 Shaun's Day Off

Field trips became a real challenge when I discovered Shaun "lifting" items he wanted from museum gift shops. He also missed a lot of school, but his mother always defended him.

One day, the police came to investigate whether or not Shaun was in school on a certain day. His mother claimed he was. He was not! The real story was a remarkable tale of just an ordinary day in Shaun's life.

This particular day, he left home and found someone's unlocked bicycle at school. He took the bike and pedaled out to a shopping center to find himself a swimming suit. He took one that he liked and then biked over to a small grocery store. There, he "found" a frozen pizza which he added to his collection and continued on his trek—the destination being the Ramada Inn. Once there, he found a place to change into his swimming suit, asked one of the cooks in the kitchen to heat up his pizza—and while he waited, went swimming.

The cook became a little suspicious and called the police. That was the end of one clever nine-year-old's ordinary day—a day on which his mother covered for him, as usual.

Martha Pechauer
Minneapolis, Minnesota

# 39 Ernie

When I came back to my room after lunch, I heard that the police had been called to pick up Ernie. He had locked himself in a classroom, threatening everyone who tried to talk to him. Then he ran through the corridors. Two days earlier he had brought a gun to school.

I saw him, scared and exhausted, running around a corner by my room. I asked him to go outside with me. He seemed relieved and stopped. It was early spring, warm and sunny, and we sat on the side steps of the school.

We talked as two people do when they share the same pain of loss; there was no difference in age, sex, or race. He talked of his mother's dying of cancer, his concern for his younger brother and sister, and of his love and hate for his father, who came back too late, still promising things a thirteen-year old didn't believe anymore. I talked of my sixteen-year-old daughter's death in a hit-and-run accident five years before, and six months later, of the separation and later divorce, from the man I loved. And of loneliness and uncertainties.

We grieved together, and thankfully, I didn't give advice. Ernie said over and over, "I will never love anyone again." I understood, and all I could say was, "Maybe…"

He had calmed down by that time; the police retreated, and Janet, our social worker, took him home.

Ernie is learning disabled...dyslexic. He had been my reading and math student for two years. Ernie's mother was a woman who looked both years younger and older than she was. She appeared strong and gentle, and loved her children very much, wanting a different life for them. A single parent, she worked long hours, but she managed to come to school for the many needed conferences. When she became ill and realized she was going to die, her fears were for her children's future, not her own.

In those days the concept of children of average or above-average intelligence failing to learn to read, write, or do math because of a learning disability was still relatively new. Ernie was a classic textbook case. His sentences had letters and words written backwards, upside down, and inside out.

In fact, Ernie was the most difficult student I ever had. The tone of my first-hour math class seemed to be set by Ernie's mood that day. At times I was relieved when he was absent; the day would go much better. Problems often started in the van on the way to school. Ernie's anxieties and feelings of inadequacy were expressed by an exaggerated "macho image"—bragging, bullying, and threatening other students, sometimes ending in fights. He was feared, teased or ignored: he had no friends. When frustrated in class, he'd rip up his paper, knock over his desk, and stomp out of the room. He was often in the time-out area.

In spite of initial protests, there were many good days. He was making progress and he was excited about each new success. In reading class he worked with Laurie, a student teacher, and for the first time, was understanding the process of decoding new words. They liked one another and Ernie seemed more relaxed than I had ever seen him.

Then one day I talked of planning a farewell party for Laurie, as the quarter was almost over. I hadn't thought to tell Ernie that Laurie's assignment with us was for a limited time. He became very angry, then sobbing, put his head down on the desk, pounding it with his fists and shouted, "That's one more person who's left me!" I remembered that so clearly a year later when his mother was dying.

His mother went into the hospital the day before Thanksgiving. I invited Ernie and his brother and sister to join my family at my sister's home for Thanksgiving dinner. I picked them up. They lived in a house where shades were always down to prevent anyone from looking in; it also kept them from seeing out. Their dog, a German Shepherd, had to be kept in the basement when anyone but the family entered the house.

They were dressed up. Ernie was wearing a too big white shirt that was his mother's idea of dressing up, not his. I had never seen him wear anything except jeans and a jean jacket. He was sporting a new hunting knife in a sheath that he said he had just bought at Sears. I admired it, then ignored it, and I was pleased that my family did the same. My nephews, about the same age as Ernie, showed them the Atari games, and between dinner and playing the Atari, I think they had a good time. Ernie's six-year-old sister, nicknamed "Pumpkin," charmed everyone.

We talked about Ernie a lot at staff meetings. What happened that day, what we could do to make tomorrow go better, and when his mother was sick, what we could do to help. We took turns preparing meals to send home. We wanted to make school the one constant thing in his life and tried hard to balance our sympathy with expectations for following rules and a regular routine. Janet visited his mother often, and was in contact with the county social worker and other agencies, often frustrated by the bureaucracy that attends welfare.

Ernie's mother died soon after his outburst at school. Ernie's father left the city with his wife and baby. Jason and Pumpkin were placed in foster homes. Ernie was left, and moved to Illinois to live with his mother's brother. His new school called for his records in a few days; he was already in trouble.

One morning about six months later I walked into our office and saw Ernie and his uncle. He had grown. He was almost six-feet tall. His head was down and he looked sad and embarrassed. His uncle, a kindly looking man in his late twenties, spoke of trying hard to make it work. But his job involved traveling, and he was finally unable to cope with the many school suspensions and problems at home.

He brought Ernie back to school, the closest thing to a home that he had. We, too, had to say no. Ernie was too old for our program, and he was enrolled in another special education program for senior high students. Janet called the county social worker, though we all knew how hard it would be to find a foster home placement for him.

I saw him at roller-skating field trips that we had together. I could tell that he was glad to see me, but the closeness that had led to our confidence in one another was gone. He assured me that he was OK and that Pumpkin and Jason were doing fine, but after a few questions I realized they were separated and didn't see one another. He was evasive about where he lived.

Then last year I heard that things were not going well. Ernie had seizures during which he became quite violent. He is now sixteen, an age at which he can quit school, and no one knows where he is. We have forty new students and I can't help but think about them when I go home. But I still think about Ernie, and I fear that someday I'll read about him in the newspaper.

Jeri Westerman
Golden Valley, Minnesota

## 40 Jerad

It was a summer morning in July when I jangled through the front door of the local bakery and found Jerad, a former student of mine, working quietly behind the smudged pastry display. He lifted his head as I came in, glanced briefly at me through the thick smell of over-sweet frostings, and then busied himself behind the register.

At that moment a speech he had once given in my class came to mind. The topic: "Where I see myself in ten years." His speech: "In jail or dead."

He just said those four words and sat down. He didn't sugarcoat it. He never did.

I recalled that some months later, after wearing out a path to the principal's office for three years, Jerad had finally boiled over. He told the principal to fuck off and then kicked the bottom pane of the exit door so hard when he left it shattered, only holding together by the reinforcement wiring inside. It was as if he wanted to leave his anger splintered in that exit for everyone to see, to make his mark, to slam the door so hard that it would shake the school off its foundation.

Whatever the motive may have been, it was the last straw, and Jerad was expelled....

As I stood in the bakery that day many years later, looking over the pastries, I tried to think of a friendly conversation-starter. Despite all his troubles, I had believed Jerad could be salvaged, that his life could be turned around if someone could find the right connection to his world. He just seemed like a caged animal to me, afraid that if he poked his head out into the sunlight, tried to open up, he'd be caught in some deadly trap.

I watched him shove his hands in and out of his apron pocket as if he were jamming shells into the gaping chamber of a shot gun. He shuffled nervously behind the register, never looking up.

I had never really seen his eyes in class either. He never said a word, just quietly floated by with his C. He drifted along that way until one day in early January, when a note came from the office. It simply read: "Jerad has entered a treatment program and will not be returning to class for an extended period of time."

When Jerad did come back, his hair was cut, his eyes were clear and his homework was done. He turned his C into an A-, participated well in class, and even engaged in small talk. He had turned it all around, I thought.

It lasted one month. Less than two months before graduation, Jerad was gone for good.

While lost in these reflections, I had moved to the front of the line. Jerad shuffled over and waited silently for my order.

"How are you doing, Jerad?" I asked, looking up at him, offering a smile. I hoped for more than four words this time.

"Livin', I guess," he said. He looked at me for the first time as he said this. I still remember his heavy eyes, sunken, as if pressed back into their sockets by the tremendous weight of his life.

I didn't have a reply. I didn't know what to say to that, so I paid for my donuts and left, but his three words have lingered with me ever since, when troubled students raise a hand or stare out my classroom window like they're looking for an answer to one of life's tough questions. They've been with me when a student is ticketed with minor consumption or busted with drugs. They've even been with me when I've tucked my own kids into bed at night.

His words have been like the bitter, persistent smell of smoke that lingers in a shirt or jacket long after the fire has been doused. It's been a smell that I've never been able to completely wash away.

Paul Beckermann
Dassel, Minnesota

# 41 Women's Issues

The "Have-You-Seen-Brian?" posters appeared in November. I saw them in grocery stores, school hallways, liquor stores, and in gas stations across northern Minnesota. Missing since Halloween night was Brian Johnson, nineteen years old. The black and white photograph, probably from high school graduation, showed a pleasant-looking, wavy-haired young man with an engaging smile. (I remember thinking, the first time I saw the poster, that my twelve-year old son would look like that at nineteen.) I had not seen Brian, but I saw his mother, Sandy, four days a week.

I had learned about Brian's disappearance halfway through the quarter. Sandy, in her late thirties, came to my office and told me the story in a quiet, steady voice that barely disguised her pain. According to friends, Brian had been at a party, had been drinking; there had been some sort of altercation with others at the party, and he left around midnight. This was the last time anyone saw him. Sandy told of the police search, the possibility of Brian falling in the river near the party scene, the difficulty of the search as the days grew colder and the snow deepened and the river froze. She told of her own search: trying to talk to Brian's friends and acquaintances to discover clues to his disappearance; trying to determine which way he walked into the thickening snow that night. "I've so little to go on," she said, "and even less from those at the party that night. They feel guilty or afraid or both. There's this wall of silence." She paused but did not break down. Did not cry.

I could only nod encouragingly, as we teachers do in office conferences with our students. I could find few words for Sandy's problem.

"This...this limbo," she said, and went on about the problems it was causing for her husband and their other children; how all of them, as the weeks passed, spent more and more time distributing posters in a wider and wider circle about Minnesota.

But I came to talk about my class-work," she said abruptly.

"Really, it's okay," I began.

"No, I apologize for my performance in class, for my lack of concentration."

I couldn't believe she was worried about missing classes, about late papers. I tried to reassure her that the class could wait, but she would have none of it. "I want to keep up," she said.

I felt tongue-tied. Inadequate.

The days and weeks passed with no news. I, too, lived under the shadow of Brian's disappearance. Every morning I scanned the newspaper for his name. At the university, Sandy daily updated me and her friends in the class, a small circle of older-than-average women students, most mothers themselves. The rest of the class, mainly eighteen- and nineteen-year-olds, went chattering out the door, unaware of Sandy's torment. I came to see the class as a microcosm of mothers and children. The year progressed. Sandy became my advisee; we kept in close touch, and as winter slowly lost its grip on us, I felt her hope fade. In May came the unthinkable news. Brian's body had been found in the river. There was a funeral, and summer came. We all had to move on.

Now autumn is here. It is nearly time for classes to start up again. As I plan my syllabus for Women's Issues, I think of Sandy and Brian. It's clear to me that having a child and losing that child is the women's issue above all others. It is also a lesson that cannot be taught.

Rosalie Weaver
Bemidji, Minnesota

# 42 Conversation in the Faculty Lounge

How can you love these children? They are so full of mistakes," says one. "It's not their fault," replies the other. "They don't know any better."

"I mean, how can you expect them to learn any history, or math? They don't even know how to sit down and listen!"

"It's not their fault. Their knees don't bend correctly and someone has broken their ears while they were asleep."

"Things have gotten so bad I don't know if I can go on much longer. I mean, how much satisfaction is there in fighting with a hundred kids a day over the Treaty of Versailles?"

"It's not their fault. When the treaty was signed, children did not count for anything. They were not considered."

George Roberts
Minneapolis, Minnesota

# 43 The Facts of Life

Valerie is not in class today. As we begin to read a short story she is outside in the school parking lot, getting into a car with an older man. What is there in a textbook that can compete with a beige Cadillac and a good-looking twenty-six-year-old guy?

The fact is that nothing, right now, will draw her back

into the classroom. The sweet smell of leather upholstery, Luther Vandross crooning from the speakers, the tingle rocketing along nerve passages as they drive away together, smiling.

She is learning the facts of life. And I am learning them too.

George Roberts
Minneapolis, Minnesota

## 44 The Token Heathen

My parent-teacher conference from Hell came at Cathedral High School. I had caught two seniors (boyfriend/girlfriend) cheating on a test. I gave both of them a zero, which ultimately lowered their grades for the quarter. During the conferences the mother of the boy apologized profusely, saying she had never raised her son that way, et cetera. Later, the father of the girl showed up. He informed me that he had attended conferences only once before (when his son had been accused of stealing). He proceeded to yell at me for about twenty minutes, telling me in one breath that I could not prove my accusations in a court of law, and in the next breath that

I should not be trying to force *my* mores on his daughter. He also thought I should allow cheating.

After unsuccessfully trying to reason with him, suggesting that I didn't need to prove anything in a court of law, and pointing out that if he didn't want any moral education for his daughter he shouldn't have sent her to a Catholic school, I walked out. He wouldn't leave, so I left.

A line of parents had been waiting to see me, and they heard every word. I went to the faculty restroom, which was located in the "dungeon," and let out a good scream to release my pent-up anger. A nun came in and calmed me down so that I could go back and face the rest of the parents. The real irony of this story is that I'm one of those "lackadaisical Lutherans," and the Catholic faculty often teased me about being their token heathen. Yet, here I stood accused of forcing my mores on a student.

Vi Ann Olson
Rochester, Minnesota

# 45 Learning to Love

When I reflect on my years of teaching and counseling at Southwest High School, I am struck more by what I learned from those I would teach than what I presumably taught. My role as "drug lady" provided many opportunities to "teach" the perils of drug abuse among adolescents, but one very poignant encounter with a young woman taught me almost everything I needed to know, and I have used her story in my teaching ever since.

Sarah (not her real name) was a daily pot smoker. She was referred to me by the school principal because her grades were slipping, she was skipping classes, and she was in trouble at home. She was deteriorating generally in her day-to-day life. Sarah came to me willingly, spoke openly of her pot use, and announced that she took great care to avoid looking like a preppie or a jock (she would rather be dead, she said). She began to come to my office regularly just to chat.

One day I proposed to Sarah that she experiment with being straight since she already knew what smoking pot was doing for her. She agreed. For three months Sarah stayed drug free. Her life improved dramatically: she did better in school, stayed in her classes, and her mom reported improvement in her home life. After three months, Sarah reported that she had resumed smoking pot. I asked her what went through her head that made going back to drug use attractive when her life was so much improved while she was straight. Sarah replied, "When I am straight, I don't have anyone to be with, and the kids who use look so stupid. But when I use, I have someone to be with and I don't care if it's stupid." What I learned from Sarah is the overwhelming scourge of loneliness and sense of isolation suffered by so many humans. Chemical abuse eases that pain and provides the deadening effect of "not caring."

In a film I show now to adult recovering chemically dependent persons, a character who is becoming alcoholic states, "I'm just an old man who's scared of life, but more afraid of dying. So I just keep on getting drunk, and then I don't give a damn."

These two people, a sixteen-year-old girl and a sixtyish old man, portray in bold relief the deepest and most devastating effects of chemical abuse: the "I don't care" response to life and all its sorrows as well as joys. This I have learned: what needs to be healed is not just the abuse of chemicals, but the inability or unwillingness to cope with sorrow and pain. People need to break down their walls of isolation and to ultimately engage in loving, authentic relationships with others.

Joan Hawkinson
Minneapolis, Minnesota

## 46 Sweating the Big Stuff

I had returned to Minneapolis on a sunny, cold day in January, 1986, from my teaching job at SSU in Marshall, MN, deep in farm country. On the spur of the moment, I stopped for a quick visit with Charlie and Kay, parents of four teenagers.

The atmosphere was thick with tension, but Charlie was delighted to draw me into a family debate. Their thirteen-year-old son, already a "ladies man," waited in the basement for the outcome.

Charlie and Kay were trying to decide whether or not their son could join a group of thirteen-year-old boys and girls for the evening. One of the girl's parents had rented a limo so they could spend the evening riding to St. Paul to see the Winter Carnival Ice Palace and enjoy a star-studded night. This was the newest way to keep kids out of the house, off the streets and out of trouble. Charlie and Kay were polling everyone who entered—should they let their son go? They wanted my opinion before stating theirs.

I cast a "no" vote. They asked why. I replied, "What would allowing such incredible self-indulgence at age thirteen teach their son about his expectations and his place in the world?"

Charlie nodded, "Exactly." Kay clearly didn't get it. I asked her why she would permit this, and she said, "Why sweat the small stuff? Save "No" for something big."

I told Kay I thought this was very big—certainly bigger than any of us at this table. I told them about the woman who had entered my office at SSU on Friday afternoon.

She was one of the non-treads (short for non-traditional students), fortyish and marked by poverty—sallow, overweight, in need of a haircut. She was also crying and trying hard to get her voice under control. She was the only student in my Intro to Theatre class who asked interesting questions.

I offered her the Kleenex box and told her to take her time. Finally, she was able to speak, "I have to quit school." The story and the tears continued. She had cashed a bad check at the grocery store and the police had come to her home. She had two weeks to make restitution or face a court hearing. I asked for more information. She and her husband owned a farm and a foreclosure notice had arrived from the bank. Her husband had done nothing for months but lie on their bed in deep depression. There was no food in the house, no money, no credit, and four young children.

She had just finished her first quarter of college and made the Dean's list. She had deferred college for years, but in their desperate situation, it was clear she needed a job that would support six people, and this meant she needed an education more than she needed good food or a haircut. But she couldn't watch her kids go hungry. She had run out of options.

At this point, the thirteen-year old emerged from the basement and asked for the decision. Charlie sent him back to the basement while more opinions were collected, this time from a couple of friends arriving to play cards. They divided along the same lines as Charlie and Kay; he was against, she was for, and their reasoning was similar. I excused myself without knowing the outcome.

To be without options is to be without hope. Then why isn't the opposite true? To have limitless options should provide limitless hope. But the logic failed; to have the option of a limo party at age thirteen left me feeling uneasy and hopeless.

Back in Marshall, my non-tread was put in touch with counselors and financial aid representatives who eventually helped her back into school.

Ten years have passed. The farm was lost as well as the marriage, but this woman has options now. The verdict still isn't in for the thirteen-year old. He is twenty-four and still not sweating the small stuff.

Sally Childs
Minneapolis, Minnesota

# 47  Of Soybeans and Stones

Many years ago, when I first became a college professor, one of my bright and talented young advisees was beginning her student teaching at a local elementary school with one of those formidable (and familiar) older teachers whose approach to just about everything had hardened into dogma. The sixth-graders were studying poetry, and my advisee was increasingly frustrated at her failure to please her supervisor, especially when she tried anything new or different.

One day my advisee came to my office in tears. Please, she begged, could I come and visit her sixth-graders, read some poems to them and talk a little about poetry? If she could bring in an "expert," she could "make some points that just might save me," as she put it.

I agreed to help, reluctantly—my first reaction was a kind of panic. The last sixth-grade class I'd been in was my own, which I'd both feared and hated. What in the world was I going to say to those kids? What could I read to them that would hold their attention?

When I visited the sixth-grade classroom the next week, even though I was armed with far more poems than I could hope to read in my allotted forty minutes, the old anxiety I had felt as a child was there immediately. The classroom itself was a bit different: movable desks instead of fixed ones, for example, and walls full of bright posters and poems the sixth-graders had been "forced to write," as one of them later told me. And the teacher, well, she was even more formidable than I'd imagined her—but also eager to tell me she always began her poetry unit with haiku, not because she liked that kind of poetry, but because it was such a good way to review *syllables* with her classes.

Finally, it was time for me to begin my presentation, and as my advisee finished her introduction, my panic began to subside. Those kids were a little smaller and quieter than I'd expected, though the back row consisted of five or six boys already squirming in their seats and casting knowing glances among themselves. I knew that everything in the next forty minutes would depend on them, and I suddenly found myself abandoning the Sandburg poem I'd planned to start with, turning instead to one by Robert Bly, a very *Minnesota* poem called "Driving toward the Lac Qui Parle River," which begins:

> *I am driving; it is dusk; Minnesota.*
> *The stubble field catches the last growth of sun.*
> *The soybeans are breathing on all sides.*

No sooner had I read that last line than hands shot up from the front row, the group of teacher-pleasers present in just about any classroom. "You can't use words like *soybeans* in a poem," they announced, almost as one. At this, the boys in the back row were nearly falling out of their seats; the teacher nodded her approval from one corner of the room, and from another, my advisee looked as though she wanted to leap through a window.

Quickly, I explained just who Robert Bly was, how he'd grown up on a Minnesota farm and had gone on to win the National Book Award. With grudging approval, the first row let me continue: more Bly, and then James Wright's "A Blessing," which begins, "Just off the highway to Rochester, Minnesota, / Twilight bounds softly forth on the grass." Someone in the front row remembered traveling to Rochester, Minnesota. I read on with increasing animation: Stafford, Dickinson, Frost. Most of the class seemed attentive, actually enjoying themselves—except for those restless boys, whispering and passing papers back and forth along the back row of desks. I tried hard not to look at them, although I couldn't help doing so, especially when the teacher moved over to stand behind them, arms folded, glowering.

When my forty minutes finally passed, the class applauded me rather enthusiastically. Some of the girls from the front row announced how much they just *loooved* poems, especially rhyming ones, and then that group of boys from the back row approached the desk as I packed up my books. Giggling, and pushing each other forward, they presented me the papers they had been writing on and passing among themselves during my reading: not notes or drawings, as I'd imagined, but soybean poems! From that first Robert Bly poem I'd read, they had gleefully been working on their own soybean poems.

I must admit I don't remember any of those poems, except for the fact that none of them were haiku, but I do remember those boys' faces, and their pride at striking a blow for literary freedom. Stunned, I stood there clutching their papers as the class formed its orderly line for the lunchroom. Several of those boys waved to me as they disappeared out the door, and I waved back, frantically, grinning like Lewis Carroll's beamish boy hoisting the head of his slain monster.

My advisee later informed me that she went on to a limited success with that teacher, and that in the process she had indeed discovered something about her own resourcefulness. I have no idea how much my visit actually helped her, but I do know how much it helped *me*. That class with the sixth-graders and that marvelous soybean breakthrough remains as important an experience as any I've had in a classroom.

Literature in the classroom can seem so remote and inaccessible if we can't find the point where it touches our own lives. If we react only as we think we must, only as habit and custom dictate, then the most important part of the experience will probably be lost—the part that moves us, that causes us to question or imagine. What frustrated

Frost's speaker in "Mending Wall" was that his neighbor could not "go behind his father's saying." As a teacher, more than anything, that is what continues to frustrate me—not just what I see in my students, but what I sometimes find in myself. If it amazes me that so many of my recent students and student writers have already learned to close themselves off to the possibilities of literature, it also amazes me how often I've found myself—whether from laziness or frustration—taking the easy path, the rigid one: what's good for you, what you must know, the way it's done. No discoveries there, no soybeans.

Mark Vinz
Moorhead, Minnesota

# Laughing

I can recall two people from my lifetime in the classroom who could not, or refused to, use or understand figurative language. One was a fifty-year-old lumberman in my poetry course who had a mental block where any sort of metaphor was concerned. To him, "A rose is a rose is a rose" though silly, was perfectly logical, but "My luv is like a red red rose," remained as incomprehensible at the end of the course as it had seemed to him at the beginning. He was beyond my help.

The other literalist was a junior in high school whose name was Marv, the sort of smart, lazy kid whose only reason for staying alert in class was to catch his teacher out in a mistake or some bit of foolishness. His instructor on the day we read Robert Frost happened to be my student teacher, a very capable young woman named Helen. She read aloud, slowly and with great feeling, Frost's "The Road Not Taken," a poem about coming to a fork in the road and deciding which one to take. It begins,

> *Two roads diverged in a yellow wood,*

and concludes,

> *I took the one less traveled by,*
> *And that has made all the difference.*

Hoping to delve into its symbolic meaning, she asked the class, "Has this ever happened to you?"

No answer.

She then addressed our obstinate literalist—I probably should have warned her about him— saying, "Marv, can you give me an example of this from your own life?"

He gave her, instead, a very dark look and turned away.

"Making a choice that seems small at the time?" she persisted. "And yet it changed the course of your life?"

He turned back to her and declared, with the tiniest hint of a smile, "I never walk in the woods."

Laughter engulfed the room. Even I, even Helen, had to laugh. Marvin's little joke was on Helen, but she laughed anyhow. When I saw her laughing, I knew she would be a good teacher. For nothing brings a class together like a good laugh. Laughter makes everyone sit up and pay attention. It's a breath of fresh air.

Jon Hassler

## 48 A Meaningful Mix-up

One more day of trying to teach English to seventh and eighth graders was almost over. Most of the students had surged out of the door just after the final bell had rung. As I picked up a stack of test papers and turned back to my desk, I realized three of my seventh grade boys were still there.

"Class was dismissed," I said. "You boys better run along home."

"Could you do it right now?" asked John. "You see, we gotta know whether our grades are good enough so we can play intramural basketball this next week."

"Please," chimed in Bobby. "It's very important. We just have to know so we can work out our plans."

They hung around my desk chattering incessantly among themselves. Finally, I said, "Look, I can't concentrate so I can get these done. Either you be quiet or go home."

Just at this moment, Walt Bristol, the principal of our department, stuck his head in the door to say "Good night." Bobby piped up and said, "Mr. Bristol, do you know what Miss Drebing is doing?"

Walt said, "No."

"She's constipating," said Bobby, "so she can get our grades ready for us."

It was amazing how many faculty members inquired about my health in the next few days.

June M. Drebing
Minnetonka, Minnesota

# 49 What's a Cotton Gin?

Here in the Midwest, where we harvest grain with a machine called a combine, we were discussing *To Kill a Mockingbird*, and one of my ninth graders stated, "We know Tom Robinson couldn't have caused the bruises on the right side of Mayella Ewell's face because his left arm had been caught in a concubine and was useless."

Struck dumb for a moment, I waited for the class to respond. One girl said, "Not a concubine, you dummy, it was a cotton gin!"

Dawn Hill
Golden Valley, Minnesota

# 50 Attentive Students

It was a fall morning; I remember, when I was taking roll, hearing the faint but earnest *boom, boom, boom* of the band practicing on the football field on the other side of the campus. I knew I was on, and the class was a good one, with everything going for it: examples, emphasis, humor. The students seemed focused, attentive.

Then we were winding down; I was summarizing, concluding with authority. Just after I had finished my last point—what timing!—the bell rang and the students stood up and began to walk past the front of the podium. I stood there waiting for someone to stop and ask me a question. Jeff, from the second row, stopped in front of me.

"Mr. Evans, you've got a leaf on the top of your head," he said.

I reached up and grabbed a large, green leaf.

"Thanks," I said.

"You're welcome," he said, and continued on past the podium with the others and out the door. I heard laughter in the hallway.

Dave Allen Evans
Brookings, South Dakota

## 51 Ms. Malaprop

During my very first parent-teacher conferences a parent hinted at the type of play I should direct.

"We should be able to understand it," she said.

"OK," I said with interest.

"It should be funny, not serious. I like real funny plays."

"Something farcical?" I suggested.

"What!"

"You know, a farce."

"Shame on you!" she exclaimed and abruptly left the room.

Gordon W. Fredrickson
Lakeville, Minnesota

## 52 The Chickens

I was asked to substitute for the principal and eighth grade teacher in the days before Thanksgiving, November 1936. Before classes began Monday afternoon, a tall, rather shy fellow who rode the street car from a Polish parish some miles away lumbered up to the front of my classroom. With his head lowered, he asked, "My mother would like to send the sisters some chickens for Thanksgiving. Would you like them alive or peeled?"

Sister Brigid Dunne, O. S. B.
Bismarck, North Dakota

# 53 Nice Girl

In the late sixties I was teaching basic drawing in the art department at the University of Minnesota. Art students had to take basic drawing before they could take other two-dimension courses and the class size was limited. Moreover, the number of basic drawing classes was always inadequate to the need, so there was pressure. I always admitted about five or six extra students because I liked a larger class and I could also select those whom I thought would be the good and eager ones. A young, very pretty girl from Cloquet, Minnesota, came to my office after I had filled the class to my quota. "Mister Egerman," she said, looking me straight in the eye, "I will do *anything...*" she paused here "...to get into your class." I believe she didn't fully know what she was saying. I let her in without hesitation; she was a nice girl and a good student. Her name was Jessica Lange.

Tom Egerman
Minneapolis, Minnesota

# 54 Animals Need Not Apply

Many years ago I directed *Fiddler on the Roof* at a high school in South Dakota. I was adamant that no plastic cups or polyester fabric be used. The students had to research the prayer shawls and the wedding ceremony to make sure we did everything correctly. The bottle dancers were to practice enough to really balance those bottles on their hats. (They did, and were rewarded with loud applause during a performance when one fell, rolled off the stage, and crashed onto the gym floor.)

A few days before the show was to open, the students came to me and asked what should be done about the chickens that were a wedding present. They had said that since I wanted everything as correct as possible, we should be using live chickens. I told them chickens would make too much noise and there were wooden cages back in those days, and we didn't have such a cage and couldn't get one in time. A little girl told me that her father could make a cage of wooden slats. The students reassured me that since everything was dark at the beginning of the scene, only lit by candles, that the chickens would be quiet. I held out as long as I could, but I was forced to give in. After all, it had been my own edict.

The night of the play the chickens arrived in a wooden

cage that was a work of art. They were quietly covered backstage and I was pleased and proud of my students' dedication. I was sure everything would work out.

The last scene of act one, the wedding scene, began. It was the painting of a Dutch master, all amber light and muted color. The bride's family entered as the groom's family came down a huge ramp that was the major set piece. Two lines of serious villagers walking in a ceremonious step-pause, step-pause began to fill the stage. All faces were lit by the dim glow of candlelight. As the song "Sunrise, Sunset" began, and the glow of fifty candles on stage moved in two perfectly choreographed lines to the center, the crowd began to giggle. The chickens had joined with their own contribution to the music. The cast sang "Sunrise.." The chickens chimed in with perfect timing, "Brock!"

> "Sunset.."
> "Brock!"
> "Sunrise.."
> "Brock!"
> "Swiftly.."
> "Brock!"
> "..fly the years."
> "Brock brock brock!"

The cast, trying not to burst into laughter, kept singing, but in stifling their giggles, blew out their candles.

(The audience roared, but the director burst into tears.) The character who had given the wedding the gift of the singing chickens slowly took off his coat and laid it over

the cage. The clucking subsided. Those whose candles had been blown out, lighted their candles from those who'd managed not to extinguish theirs, and gradually the scene resumed its beauty, dignity, and grace. Although a few laughs could be heard at each "Sunrise, Sunset" refrain, the audience helped the cast get things under control.

I continue to direct student musicals, but I am now adamant that NO ANIMALS are 'cast'.

Louise Bormann
Bloomington, Minnesota

# 55 Universal Needs

While attending a pre-school workshop in Long Prairie, Minnesota, I was armed with all the information that my college Education courses could give me. When the Principal said, "Wednesday night is church night in this community," I made a mental note never to schedule any school events on that night. There were many other things to remember but this one was very concrete and something I knew I'd better not violate.

When school started and the students were actually in front of me I was deep into my lessons but my mind was also full of all those rules that I had to remember. We were studying the Amazon Rainforest and looking at the people of this region. I noted that in these equatorial regions the basic needs of the people for food, shelter and clothing were the same as any other place in the world. These needs may be secured in different ways but all societies and cultures needed them. And this was true all over the world.

I looked for reaction and saw several heads nod in agreement. To carry the lesson one step further, I then asked the class, "What other things do these people have in common with other cultures all over the world?" I was hoping for someone to say, 'Religion.'

The class sat riveted on me. The students seemed to be thinking about the lesson but not one word was uttered.

Again I said, "What do we do here in Long Prairie that people also do in Europe and in the Amazon Rainforest? Think! Think! Think about your life here."

Still no response.

Finally, I offered a broad hint, "It happens in this community on Wednesday night."

I looked out over the seventh grade class looking for a light to go on above someone's head. Finally, one student in the back of the room opened his hand and stabbed the sky with that "oh! oh!" sound under his breath.

I quickly called on him. "Larry," I said.

"Roller skating," he answered.

Robert E. Werschay
St. Cloud, Minnesota

# 56 Dr. D

Having just been married and with the first child on the way, the realities of life were becoming all too clear to this young man who had been dreamily attending graduate school for the past two years. As winter quarter approached, the specter of student teaching began to loom up ahead of me like some iceberg in a foggy sea of part-time jobs and night classes.

It was at this time that a stroke of real good fortune came to me by way of a phone call from a former teacher of mine at St. Paul Academy, where I had graduated six years earlier. He needed someone to teach two of his classes so he could devote more of his time to his administrative duties at the school. Would I be interested, he wanted to know. And incidentally, my teaching at SPA could qualify as student teaching, as well as provide some needed dollars.

What a perfect situation and what a gift. Naturally, I jumped in with both feet. As the days and weeks went by, I got over the initial awkwardness and really began to like the kids and the material. I began to think I was doing the job and that this "teaching" wasn't so tough after all. The only fly in this pedagogical ointment was that I had to be observed by my supervising teacher, Dr. Richard B. Dierenfield. So strong grew my confidence, some might say arrogance, that not even the prospect of this dreaded confrontation dampened my enthusiasm. I hardly listened to stories of my fellow apprentice teachers' sweat and stress and final relief when this last hurdle had been cleared. No big deal; I was cool and it was all going to be just fine.

The students were alert and ready. Dr. D. entered, was introduced, and took his place in the back corner of the room to my right. As I readied myself for the distribution of rare insights into the depths of *The Great Gatsby*, Dr. D. activated his tape recorder and prepared his notebook.

The hour passed. And what an hour it was; the students were rapt; I was profound; Jay Gatsby was alive in our midst and by the time the ending bell rang, Dr. Dierenfield had fallen fast asleep.

In the years since, I have put many a student to sleep with much less effort, but never have I encountered anyone more apologetic upon awakening. Amid the scramble to get his notes and tape recorder and jacket all in order, and to escape from my perplexed bewilderment, the poor professor could find no words to assuage the moment.

To say that I immediately dropped out of school, burned my AFT card and opened a very successful Greek restaurant, might be appropriate because all these and many other thoughts stormed my mind that day. However, one chapter does not make a book, nor one day a life. I have labored on with fine days in the classroom too numerous to count. And even now, when I run into Dr. D in the hardware store, the memory we share of that day is very rich.

George Vasiliou
Eagan, Minnesota


# 57 Reminiscing

I can remember getting a note from a mother asking me to excuse her son from school because he had a pain in his growth bone.

Or the time we got new band uniforms and I "assigned" some band girls to reinforce the sewing on the uniform citation cords, and they also sewed the jacket sleeves and pant cuffs of my uniform shut (before I put it on, that is) which left me in the men's lounge pulling thread to get my uniform on while the bus waited.

When I was a counselor at Edison High School, Minneapolis, I came home one Friday night to find my house TP'd—very artistic job, nice bows on the porch light, trim along the flower bed, etc. I admired it in the moonlight and went to bed—I could take it down in the morning. Shortly after retiring I heard some activity outside, and peeking out the window I saw a group of seniors taking it all down. While they were struggling to reach the last piece out of a tree I called out the window for them to just leave it—they fled. On Monday, some sheepish faces peeked around the door of my office. I told them they had done a beautiful job and asked them why they'd come back to take it down. They explained that they were afraid I had gone for the weekend and that the neighbors would be mad if it stayed up until I got back.

Or another band story. After playing at the Minnesota State Fair for three days the busses got us back in the early evening. I had hardly gotten home when the doorbell rang. There was a student with a cold can of beer. She said her mother sent her over with it and that she thought that I just might need it about now.

Al Sweat
Edina, Minnesota

## 58 Mouths of Babes

A first grader (Kris) whose parents had signed him up for soccer, swimming, hockey, etc. when he was in kindergarten, attempted to leave school at noon, thinking he only had to attend a half day as he had in kindergarten. When the teacher said, "Kris, you can't go home yet," he replied, "'What in the hell did they sign me up for now?"

Faye H. Thiel
Cloquet, Minnesota

## 59  Department Chair

When teaching at Cathedral High School I also served on the faculty negotiations committee. At one meeting with the board's committee I presented our proposal for salaries. One board member proceeded to double-check my calculations, only to conclude that they were correct. The superintendent said, "She's not the chair of our math department for nothing." The board member responded with "We have women in our math department? I didn't know that!" I then informed him that his daughter was in my class.

Vi Ann Olson
Rochester, Minnesota

# 60  Maternity Leave

It was not easy, I'd heard, to get into the Oak Harbor school system, but now I had won the job to replace Judy Lender, taking maternity leave sometime in February. I had only to wait until she called for me!

My daily walks often took me near the school, and from the sidewalk I peered toward Mrs. Lender's windows, trying to appear casual while hoping to get a glance inside to learn how things were run. It was obvious, even from that distance, that there was a certain regimentation common in a first-grade classroom. The cubes for math were sorted by color and bordered the window sill like spring flowers; red, blue, yellow, maroon, orange, green. What happened to the brown and black? Not enough room on the sill? She must have stowed them below on a shelf.

The call came at eight in the evening. I was at choir practice at church and someone from the office announced I was wanted on the phone.

It was Mrs. Lender. She introduced herself and said she wanted to give me a few instructions that she had neglected to write in the red folder on the desk. First of all, Matthew was not to begin his Friday math as the work in his file must be completed before he moves on and that his orange file was the third one in the pile on the cabinet next to the sink in the rear of the room.

Next, it was crucial that Alexis finish her artwork (the green paper on the heater) BEFORE recess as the aide would be framing them and it must be. . . .

Mrs. Lender cut the directions off with a "one moment, please" and then I heard the heavy breathing. Controlled, rhythmic breathing. In and hold. Out with a whish.

I waited and listened. Oh, heavens. She was in labor! I recognized that breathing from my second child. I had scanned the book, *Six Practical Lessons for an Easier Childbirth*, by Elizabeth Bing the night before Steven arrived. It all came back to me—the forced breathing and staring at a spot on the wall. I wondered if Mrs. Lender was concentrating on a tiny crack or a bug on her wall. I hoped she had read the book more thoroughly than I. It sounded as if she was in control.

Then a pause. She continued with the directions for Alexis. After filling me in on the precise duties of the aide, I was directed toward Benjamin, who had misplaced his phonics folder, and would I please look under the front table where the new spelling curriculum was waiting because he must complete page forty-seven before Monday?

Mrs. Lender asked me to hold on, and then it started again. The whistling sounds, in and out. I mysteriously felt an empathetic pressure on my pelvic floor. She finished and asked if I knew how to use an ice-cream maker and could I pick up ice on the way to school in the morning? Her husband would be dropping off the machine and the children were all assigned ingredients to bring for the promised Valentine Day party.

Instantly, I had dramatic visions of twenty-eight children parading into the room, clutching bags of cream, vanilla flavoring, sprinkles, and rock salt, asking for Mrs. Lender while I herded Matthew, Alexis, and Benjamin to their respective "musts."

The picture was frantic. I needed to do some deep breathing myself.

"Mrs. Lender...please, please...tell your husband we won't need the ice-cream maker, and don't you worry about a thing. I think *you* should go have a baby!"

Paddy O'Callaghan Myer
Yakama, Washington

## 61 Teaching Too Long

I am a native Nebraskan, so I pride myself in knowing most of the towns, even the really little ones, in the state. I also can often identify where the college students come from simply by learning their surnames, for one does come to associate certain family names with certain locales in the state.

One first day in a semester I asked a girl what her last name was, and she told me it was "Martindale."

"Oh," I said, "from Brewster?"

"That's right," she said, and she was a little amazed at the connection I had drawn from her name.

"I think I had your mother in one of my classes," I said. "Elaine, isn't it?"

"Oh," she replied, "that's my grandmother."

At such times I realize how long I have been teaching.

Vern Plambeck
Kearney, Nebraska

# 62  Big John and the Little Mouse

The building that houses my classroom was built back in 1934 and has had several generations of field mice call it home. It's not that anybody noticed them that much, but you knew they were there. Little gray bodies dashing between the radiators; beady little eyes peering out at us as we struggled with Shakespeare or Poe; speedy little feet relaying back and forth on the dropped ceiling as we delved deeper into the importance of grammar in our daily lives.

These mice were educated mice. They had the run of the building: English to math, math to the library, the library to business education. Our whiskered friends knew their school and all of its do's and don'ts. Rule Number One: Stay Away From People. I could almost see little teacher mice instructing their charges in this most important of all life skills. I could also see that some of these student mice slept through their lessons.

Such was the case with one truant mouse. For about a week, my classroom had been plagued with a bold daredevil who had abandoned the safe hideaways of his cousins to journey to and fro among the students' desks, leaving screaming and jumping teenagers in his wake. It reached the point that many of my students would not put their feet on the floor during class. Instead, they placed their feet on the chair legs of the desks in front of them.

Then the little critter met up with John Paul.

John Paul Davis was a redneck legend in our school. He couldn't pass anything, and he hated school, but the boy could drink. A weekend didn't pass without a story about how much beer or whiskey John Paul had put away. As a result, he spent most of his Mondays hung over.

When John Paul was hung over, no one messed with him. Teacher or student—man or beast—only a fool got in the way of this large, wood-chopping, beer drinking, teenage alcoholic.

No one, that is, except the daredevil mouse.

First, the mouse would dash one way, then he dashed the other. Each pass brought him closer to John Paul, his dragging tail insulting the sullen giant like an upraised middle finger.

Class came to a halt. All eyes were on the furry intruder. We were in awe of his arrogance, his bravery, his …

Splat! John Paul struck. His heavy work boot smashed the tiny mouse into the floor. A seeping puddle of blood oozed out from under his heel. The reckless mouse was no more.

Big John slowly lifted his foot off the carcass revealing a smashed grey object. Most of the creature's blood ran out of its nose, mouth and ears. The mouse executioner looked down on his trophy and then up at me and asked, "Can I throw this away?" His stubby fingers picked up the mouse by its tail. Oohs and Ahs moaned through the classroom.

"Yeah, go ahead and toss it outside." I didn't want it in my waste can.

John Paul smiled as he bore the corpse through the door. He was getting out of class.

Jeffrey W. Jones
Burfordville, Missouri

# 63  Lasting Lessons

Several years after I'd left my teaching job in Hibbing, Minnesota, I was walking in downtown Hibbing and I sighted one of my old students. I introduced myself and this young man, now about twenty-years-old, said he remembered me.

I asked him what part of my World Geography he remembered most. In my mind I was thinking probably Latin America, or maybe the Soviet Union, or possibly India and South Asia. I watched his eyes dart to the sky as his mind searched the corners of his mind for "the" lesson or activity that impressed him.

He thought for a moment and finally said, "When you pulled the roll-map down, then turned around, and the map snapped back up and came right off the wall. I thought the darn thing was going to hit you in the head."

Robert E. Werschay
St. Cloud, Minnesota

# 64  A Pint of Rye

Of all the professions, it's teaching, I think, which best marks a person's time on earth, dividing life into class hours, semesters and years. We teach the children, then their children, and finally our first students appear again, gray-headed, holding the hands of their grandchildren.

The Hoffman Public School was never large, forty students a record graduating class. An older high school building and newer elementary were joined at the gymnasium. Students of all ages mingled in the hallways.

Now the high school is gone. The elementary converted to apartments. Retired teachers joke they can still get their old rooms back and live in them until they die.

In 1963, in the fourth period study hall, a half-filled pint bottle of rye whiskey appeared mysteriously in a teacher's middle desk drawer. The teacher was not amused, even after removing the cap and sniffing only tea.

Was someone implying the teacher drank? Had he in fact been seen drinking? Teachers in Hoffman drank in basements or drove to nearby towns where they weren't well known.

Red-faced, the teacher plunked the bottle onto the principal's desk. The principal held study hall in session after the bell to investigate the strange occurance, meeting row upon row of blank faces. One young lady theorized maybe the bottle had been in the desk for months. A sophomore suggested the study hall teacher really was a drunk trying to cover up.

The matter was taken to higher authority, Superintendent Kermit Klienbosser. Klienbosser ran a tight ship and was blessed with an organized mind and the courage of quick action. Classes were cancelled and the entire student body, grades seven through twelve, assembled in the gymnasium.

Mr. Klienbosser stood before them on the highly polished gym floor, the silk thread in his golden-brown suit ablaze in afternoon sunshine. He knew that somewhere among this restless throng of students his culprit lurked, undetected, maybe even confident. He must ferret that person out by force of word and personality. We faculty too, were assembled, shuffling near the free-throw line, more apprehensive than the students and convinced they wouldn't betray their own.

Mr. Klienbosser began in a reasonable tone, speaking broadly of the school's educational goals and its hopes for shaping the minds and morals of youth. We of the faculty had heard this speech before. So had the students, hunched in stoic silence as Klienbosser strode up and down the gleaming tile floor.

He then proposed that the students think it over and rat out their offending classmate. The room fell strangely silent and we all listened to the ticking of the large gym clock inside its wire cage. No one confessed.

"What is the matter with you people? Do you want anarchy to rule this school?"

The student body sat above in complete silence. No catcalls. Hardly a giggle. If Klienbosser hadn't achieved much as a detective, he'd miraculously revolutionized the usual mayhem of student assembly. If this pleased him, it didn't show.

Mr. Klienbosser's face had gone from tan to cream to raw scarlet. "All right, then," he said in a strange high voice. "You've made your choice. You won't give me the name? You worship this person? Why don't you just fall down on your faces then and worship?" He dropped to his knees. "Bow down! Worship!" He stretched his arms toward the mercury lamps and chanted, "I worship you! I worship you!" Overcome, he fell forward, arms outstretched, and bowed before them, knees square on the red foul line. Several faculty averted their eyes and the kindergarten teacher bit her lip.

After what seemed an eternity, Mr. Klienbosser arose and strode from the gymnasium.

That afternoon, the guilty party, a small and fairly quiet senior girl, surrendered herself to the principal and was ushered into Mr. Klienbosser's office, where she explained to him that she didn't want the rest of the school to suffer for her indiscretion. Vindicated, he dismissed her with a lenient punishment, but confiscated the half-pint of tea.

Several weeks later Mr. Klienbosser was visited by Ethel Elmquist and Anna Berg, two zealous members of the Women's Christian Temperance Union. The WCTU had kept hard liquor out of Grant County and recently forced pool hall owners to install heavy curtains. If the sin of pocket pool and 3.2 beer was allowed in Hoffman, at least it would be private.

When the WCTU ladies entered the superintendent's office they found it empty. Mr. Klienbosser had stepped out to the restroom in anticipation of a lengthy and exasperating visit. What they did find was something almost beyond belief.

Ethel's eyes were riveted to the second shelf behind Mr. Klienbosser's desk. "Do you see that?" she hissed.

Anna gasped. A bottle of whiskey. Half empty. "He doesn't even bother to hide it," she exclaimed.

Not only was the man a drunkard but proud of it.

They marched from the office single file down the street to a Lutheran minister's parlor, where they reported their discovery over tea.

Edna Birkmeyer Olsen
Hoffman, Minnesota

# 65 Famous Quotations

During the 1963-1964 school year, I taught high school English in Madrid, Iowa, a town of several hundred people. The school library had enough copies of that old chestnut, *Silas Marner*, to go around, and I assigned it to my ninth grade students as outside reading and gave them a couple of weeks to complete it. Then I prepared an essay exam to determine if they had indeed read the book. One of my questions was, "Based upon the physical details in the novel, how was life in the nineteenth century different from life today?" I wanted them to have noticed the coal fires, the oil lamps, travel by horse and cart, and so on.

In the class was a boy named Billy Freeman. His classmates called him "The Mole" because he had small dark eyes and a pointed nose and kept his tiny hands clenched over his heart. Billy's answer to that question was a single sentence that I have remembered for more than thirty years, "The nineteenth century did and was a lot of things different that we don't do and have of today."

Ted Kooser
Garland, Nebraska

# 66 Professor Swift

Back in the 1970s, when smoking cigarettes was still tolerated in Minnesota, I taught British literature at a small Lutheran college in Minneapolis. Lots of Lutheran faculty members smoked, because it wasn't as bad as drinking. Still others abhorred smoking and one of them told me that if God had intended me to smoke, he'd have equipped me with a chimney in my forehead. At the time, I smoked, I drank, and I was only nominally a Lutheran. Sort of a fish out of water.

I also taught a course in which the centerpiece was Jonathan Swift's *Gulliver's Travels*, a scathingly funny satire on the manners and morals of England—and of mankind in general—in the eighteenth century and for all time.

It was winter semester and my eighteenth-century British literature class met in a drafty old church on the edge of campus, a crumbling pile of moldering lathe under dingy plaster, a virtual firetrap bedecked in tinder-like wainscoting. But in those days there were no "Thank You For Not Smoking" signs as is common in Minnesota these days. So I puffed away contentedly on my Marlboros one Monday morning as I guided my class through the wondrously corrupt maze of Lilliputian life. Every time I lit up, a sniff of repulsion would emanate from some beautiful blonde Scandinavian maiden sitting in the back row doing her nails. Or possibly a veiled glance of disgust from an earnest pre-seminarian sitting in the front row, wondering how I could be so enthusiastic about Jonathan Swift, "… an Anglican for gracious sakes and latitudinarian to boot! And those cigarettes. Wood's going to set this holy house on fire!"

As Book I closes, Lemuel Gulliver gets crosswise with the tiny country's royal family. The royal palace is on fire! What to do? Gulliver knows. Gulliver stands high above the raging inferno and urinates on it, putting the fire out immediately. Do the King and Queen thank him for his quick thinking, for his saving their lives? Not on your life. They think his actions are unseemly and move quickly to eliminate him. So Gulliver bids a not-too-fond farewell to his adopted country and the hour is up. I bid my own fond farewell to the students, most of them still tittering over the urination scene.

We reconvened on Wednesday for our imaginary trip to Brobdingnag. It's one of my favorite sections because Gulliver gets his comeuppance, finds out that the giants are morally superior, making him, a mere human, feel like a "little odious vermin." So I lit up my Marlboro and we discussed the huge pores on the breasts of Glumdalclitch, our hero's nursemaid and guardian. When the first cigarette burned down, I snubbed it out on the inner edge of the wastebasket, as was my custom.

Suddenly, the wastebasket burst into flame, igniting discarded excuse slips and last Friday's pop quizzes. As the flames leaped several feet into the air, I lost whatever composure I ever had, which wasn't much.

"What should I do?" shout I. "What shall I DO!?"

"Why don't you do what Gulliver did last Monday?" asked the earnest pre-sem student, as a hockey player calmly got up, picked up the raging wastebasket, opened a window and tossed it outside into a big snowdrift, where it spluttered and sizzled and went out, sort of like the Lilliputian castle royal.

And my class? They laughed polite Lutheran laughs, more telling than gales of laughter at the old City College of New York.

Turned out that Ed, one of the class's droller students, had come to class early and laced the bottom of the basket with a can of Zippo lighter fluid. All it took was one spark from my cigarette to make me feel like one of the most "odious vermin that nature ever suffered to crawl upon the surface of the earth"—to quote one of my favorite authors.

Dave Wood
River Falls, Wisconsin

# 67 Shannon

After graduating from college, a friend and I both landed second-grade positions at Annunciation in Minneapolis. I'll never forget an incident that occurred during that very first year. (It was 1987.)

Sara and I had set up reading tables in the back of our classrooms with books and corresponding tapes to be listened to silently, using individual earphones. Sara was challenged that year by Shannon, a large, rotund eight-year-old boy with bright red hair and eyes containing a glint of mischief. One morning Sara was delighted to observe how well her group of readers at the back table was working. She complimented herself on what a good (book) choice "Little Bear's Visit" was. She even caught Shannon in a positive leadership role, making eye contact with the other students at the table, and every few minutes saying, "Now turn the page, everyone!" The students listened and followed along so intently!

During clean-up, however, the group forgot to remove the tape. It wasn't "Little Bear's Visit" they had been listening to, but the rock group Duran, Duran.

Christine M. Boerner
Watertown, Minnesota

## 68 Linguistics 101

Whenever I teach a language course, I challenge my students to find in their own speech patterns possible examples for classroom discussion. One day, as I was about to call such a discussion to order, a young woman strolled into the classroom, stopped short of her desk, looked down at her expensive new penny loafer and exclaimed, "Oh shit, I stepped in dog poop." My class in language usage was off to a fine start.

W. Dale Brown
Grand Rapids, Michigan

## 69 Cribbing

It was a typical day in high school English II. We were having a written test on a memorized piece from *Julius Caesar*. In those days girls wore skirts to school and panty hose had not yet come on the market.

As the students were writing out the soliloquy, I noticed something suspicious in the middle of the class.

I slowly made my way to the back of the room, glancing here and there, trying not to pay undue attention to one girl in particular.

By the time I reached the back of the room my suspicions were further aroused. I noticed that the girl in question was slowly pulling her skirt higher and higher on her thigh. Then I saw it. She had very carefully written the Shakespearean selection on the leg of her white long-line panty girdle.

Not being a complete fool I quietly went across the hall and got a female teacher. She handled the situation for me and the poor young lady failed the test.

Dennis Haney
Mandan, Norton Dakota

## 70 Apology

A year or two ago, in a particularly reticent freshman poetry class—one whose attention I had a very hard time holding—I received the following comment on an end-of-term student evaluation: "I really appreciate your commitment to what you do and I have to say how I'm sorry I didn't speak up in class more. I'm really sorry this whole class stayed so quiet. I don't understand why that happened. I guess we just took you for granite."

Mark Vinz
Moorhead, Minnesota

## 71 Youth and the City of Light

As a high school French teacher, I prepared students (and myself) for journeys to places pictured in our textbooks. We practiced the currency exchange with francs. We discussed the consumption of beer and wine (allowed with parental consent and only with meals, and during the buttery omelets and glasses of Alsatian beer). The students absorbed more than even they thought they could about history, geography, and cultural differences.

The scary topic of "The Family Stay" was discussed at great length. Each student was to be placed with a family and would have to communicate only in French. We role-played, talked about worst-case scenarios, and discussed Minnesota gifts to be offered upon arrival. We read the "welcome" letters that came dribbling in. I reassured those who hadn't received letters that they, too, would have loving homes to live in for six days.

I sat next to Rick in the plane from Minneapolis to Chicago. The exuberance from this diminutive high school junior was remarkable. Normally, he was shy and not very social. He reached into the pocket of his brown cloth jacket and pulled out several hundred dollars that his grandmother had slipped into his hand just before he boarded. He said that with all of the other money he had (traveler's checks and cash francs) he would not have to worry about survival during our fifteen days in France. I expressed my happiness at his good fortune and suggested keeping the bulk of it in a very safe place.

The morning of our second day in Paris, Rick came to me, downcast. His hair was slicked back in an unfamiliar style, shiny with goo, and he was wearing a new black leather jacket, tight black jeans, and Italian shoes. He told me that he had no money left and he didn't know how he was going to eat for the next thirteen days. I reminded him that minus the six days with his family, where he would be fed, he had only to worry about seven days of famine.

He didn't appreciate my humor, so I gently encouraged him to divulge his expenditures.

He had purchased many leather jackets as gifts to send home along with trinkets of all sorts. When he saw prices, he said, he simply counted out his francs, as if they were Monopoly currency.

I suggested that he live on bread and water for a day or two until his parents could wire him some more money. I didn't think that was too harsh. After all, people often fly to France just to experience the delicious bread.

Erik had also taken up smoking. At breakfast the next morning, he appeared in his black leather jacket and sauntered into the dining room, affecting combined postures of Charles Boyer and Marlon Brando. He slid into a chair at a table with six French tourists and brought out his pack of Marlboros. Clumsily, but with an obvious effort toward finesse, he lit a cigarette. He drew in the smoke, suppressed a small cough, and waved the match high in the air to extinguish the flame. The flame did not go out, however. It continued to burn in an ashtray full of butts and ashes. Erik blew out the expanding flame with a robust puff of his breath, at which point his table mates slowly looked up at him with burning stares. Their croissants were covered in soot, and gray flecks floated in their cafés au lait.

Early the following morning our touring bus took us to Normandy. We were driven to the center of a large parking lot in Arromanches, near the English Channel. The forty-five students fidgeted like fish in a tiny bowl, for surrounding the bus were the faces of strangers who would soon be whisking them away for six days. As we called each name, one student at a time walked up the aisle, shot us a final glance that said "Help!" and slowly descended the four steps to meet his new family.

Rick's turn was next. I looked toward the back of the bus and saw large, dark circles under his eyes. They were so pronounced. Poor kid, I thought, he must not have slept all night for worrying about this moment. As he approached the front, I saw that the black smudges were from makeup (some girls had applied eye liner to his lower lids and it didn't seem to be waterproof). No time to fix it. His new family would have to deal with it. Perhaps they would consider him to be an aspiring circus performer.

I spent those six days in the area, on call in case of emergency. But there were no calls. On the seventh day, we collected our charges. There were tears, farewells, and head counts. The bus roared out of the parking lot while the students hung out of windows, waving at their families who flashed us the victory sign and blew kisses.

The kids sat back, dried their tears, and chatted with teenaged animation about their individual experiences. Soon all was quiet. They slept, spent from emotion. I looked back at Rick, whose scrubbed face and pink cheeks were snuggled into the collar of his black leather jacket.

Connie Szarke
Mound, Minnesota

# Two More Stories

We conclude with two longer stories that don't precisely fit our anthology but which are too compelling to leave out. By coincidence, both stories come from the same monastery in St. Joseph, Minnesota, the first a tragic tale told by Sister Kristin Malloy, the second, altogether happier, told by Sister Andre Marthaler. But they have more in common than their source; they are stories told in retirement by two women about a period in their live that ended decades ago and yet had a profound effect on their careers. Sister Kristin gives us a horrifying account of her banishment from her college classroom by a cruel and vindictive administration. Sister Andre shows how a single unorthodox teacher in the village of West Union, Minnesota, could awaken the curiosity of a fifth grade girl and instill in her a lifelong love of teaching and learning.

Jon Hassler

# 72 The Bishop, the Chaplain, and the Wicked Nuns

It was Palm Sunday of 1958 when I was summoned to Parlor One of our convent in St. Joseph, Minnesota, and there found our prioress, Mother Richarda, in a very angry state. With her sat Sister Remberta, the president of the college; Sister Johanna, the academic dean and the chair of our English Department (of which I was a new, young member); and Sister Mariella Gable, one of the most renowned Catholic literary critics of her time. Our chaplain, Father Jerome Dougherty, a transplanted Australian living temporarily on the nearby campus of St. John's University, was also present.

"How did those books get into this house?" Mother Richarda demanded to know. She was speaking of the great number of paperback books which Sister Remberta and I, at Sister Mariella's suggestion, had bought at a nearby book wholesale house and offered for sale on campus, because our bookstore sold only textbooks, missals, and chapel veils. Mother Richarda's inquiry was motivated by Father Jerome Dougherty, who, at the behest of the Bishop of the Diocese of St. Cloud, had been on the lookout for a reason to punish Sister Mariella. (The bishop's motivation is another story entirely; he assumed that she, as a published author, was guilty of the sin of "intellectual pride.")

Mother Richarda's focus was on one particular book, J. D. Salinger's *Catcher in the Rye*—a book reported by one of our students, who'd read it the year before, to be "awful" and "terrible." And yet it was a book no student was obliged to buy, since it wasn't being taught in any of our classes. To Father Jerome, who believed that the mission of a Catholic college was "to teach students to read sacred scripture," and who later told me that "no one can read sacred scripture and at the same time read contemporary fiction," this was the break he was waiting for. He proposed a campus-wide witch hunt.

"We'll have a public burning of all such books," he said. As for the culprits, Sister Mariella and myself, he forbade us to receive the sacraments until we had confessed to this "terrible sin."

Next he required that I make a retraction in my classes, taking back everything good I'd said about the book. As I did so, he stood outside my classroom listening, and at the end of the day told me that I was much too easy on myself. My plea to the students was this: "The chaplain has the authority to ask us to cooperate. Please bring back the books I sold you." No one brought back a single book.

Father Jerome was desperate. He was furious. I finally offered to go to each student's room to collect all novels that Jerome would condemn. The dean of women, a sister, went with me. No student door had a lock or key!

The few students we found at home would say, "Here's my Shakespeare, Sister! His language is really sexy at times. And here's my Old Testament. You'll find pretty raw stuff in some of those stories. Here's my Chaucer, the raciest language you'll find." When we brought him nothing significant from our campus-wide search, Father Jerome was certain that students had hidden their copies of Salinger.

During the summer I was required to see him every day, because I was "salvageable," if only I could be gotten out from under the influence of Sister Mariella, who avoided him altogether. I recall the day Father Jerome told me how Bishop Peter Bartholome had assigned him to the very task he was now struggling to perform so perfectly: "The world is creeping onto the campus at St. Benedict's. You go out there and put a stop to it. Watch out for Sister Mariella Gable; she's known to be anti-clerical and to further pornographic writing."

Before long I refused to see Father Jerome unless Mother Richarda was there to witness what he said, and Mother Richarda refused to see him unless I was there. "Sister dear," he said to me one day in late summer (He always called me "Sister dear,") "you have not done enough penance for your sin." It seems he had actually been reading the dreaded book, but could not finish it. He complained that visions from the book kept booming around in his head day and night. For relief, he said, he had to go back to the Greeks and read some of the ancient plays, though he forbade me to teach *Medea* as "not fit for young women."

He told us that he had gone to the abbot at St. John's and made him listen to snatches of the book. The abbot had said, "You have to go to the bishop with this." Mother Richarda, too, paid a visit to the abbot, asking for another monk to replace Father Jerome. The abbot was receptive to this idea and a replacement was agreed upon. The bishop, however, overruled the abbot and Jerome stayed on. An old sister friend of mine told me she was serving a meal to the chaplain and a guest when she overheard Father Jerome say, "Either the three of them go or I go." This was my first hint that I would be sent into exile. The third one he referred to was Sister Thomas, my good friend, whose sin had been to say to Father Jerome one day, "Father, Sister Kristin is a sincere person; she is trying to do what you want, and besides, the students at St. John's are reading that book." He replied. "No Johnnie worthy of the name would be caught dead reading that book." Which was untrue. But Father Jerome went to Mother Richarda and complained, "Sister Thomas is indulging in foul mud-slinging."

By this time Mother Richarda, desperate to silence the man and come to some sort of closure, asked me to make severe public penance, or a public confession. I finally agreed: "I will do a severe public penance if I must but I can't make a speech."

"You could read it," Father Jerome suggested eagerly.

Mother Richarda agreed. "Write it and bring it to me in the morning." We were to have a chapter meeting the next day; everyone who could walk would be there.

I replied "I know I can read it, I can read it well. But I can never again sit across the table from those dear sisters at the dining table. What will they think when I tell them how terrible I am?"

I've never known what became of my statement. The next day, just as we were all about to go to our chapter meeting, and I was about to read my statement and thus end my life as a sister, Mother Richards sent for me and said, "I just had a phone call. Not all of our sisters out on the missions can attend, so we'll have to meet next week instead." She repeated this excuse every week all summer, and thus I was never forced to read my confession. At the end of the summer, however, I was sent into exile, assigned to teach at Cathedral High School in St. Cloud. This wasn't such a hardship because Cathedral was a great school. After five years there, however, I was asked to move to the village of Pierz, Minnesota, where a new Catholic high school had been recently built. Oh dear, I thought, this is really the pits—Pierz has no train, no bus, no nothing. But I had taken the vow of obedience, and so I began packing. Upon first entering my classroom in Pierz, I looked out the window and there was the cemetery. I was suddenly back in Thornton Wilder's *Our Town*. I was Emily. "Now,

Emily, just settle down and after while you'll feel at home here." And I did. We had a wonderful school in Pierz, and I served as principal during my last three years there.

My exile lasted ten years. In 1968, I returned to my home convent and campus as an assistant to the new vice-president for development, responsible for raising friends, freshmen, and funds. I held this job for thirteen years, until Sister Emmanuel, president of the college, asked if I would return to the classroom. She said she could no longer ignore the complaints of alumnae I'd taught who insisted that I should still be teaching. "I will give you a week to think it over," said Sister Emmanuel. "I don't need ten minutes," I said, and I hugged her. I was given a year's sabbatical at Oxford University, and then, in 1983, after twenty-five years away, I returned to the classroom.

Sister Mariella had been sent to Mt. Angel College in Oregon to teach in 1958 and the next two years to the Sister Formation College in Missouri. When she was finally allowed to set foot on our campus, Mother Richarda made it clear that she could teach only Dante, Chaucer, and Shakespeare. Sister Thomas was sent to our hospital in Ogden, Utah. After a year, she arrived in St. Paul, assigned to establish an Art Department in the Priory's new high school. The assigned area had no running water. Two years later she arrived in Cold Spring, eight miles from St. Benedict's, again to establish an art department. Again there was no running water. When he saw her paintings, the new lay president at the College of Saint Benedict, Stanley Idzerda, asked to have her return to teach art at the college. She had been away for ten years.

Even Father Jerome was eventually assigned to another post. His brother monks tell me they never saw him at the abbey again. He died a few years later.

Nor did anyone hear or read a public account of the *Catcher* case. I consistently refused to be interviewed for student newspapers seeking it. Jon Hassler and Robert Spaeth, dean of St. John's University, asked me to write it in 1993, but I put it off. Only in 1996, when Nancy Hynes revealed the basis of the story in *The Literature of Spiritual Values and Catholic Fiction*, did I agree to tell the whole thing. I told it to the English Club and English faculty in October, 1996. I agreed to tell it to a roomful of our sisters at the request of the Prioress early in 1997. Hearing it for the first time, they were stunned. I did tell it this year at lunch at the Chancery office at the invitation of our Bishop, John Kinney—a perfect audience, for me a blessing, a healing hour.

I tell it now as a part of our community's history and, even more, to suggest the price we pay for the "oppression of silence."

Kristin Malloy, OSB
St. Joseph, Minnesota

# 73 An Amazing Teacher

All of my adult life I have wanted to tell the story of one of the most unconventional teachers I ever had. No one teacher influenced my attitudes, my methodology, and my passion for the teaching profession more than did this woman.

Lydia Ann DeLaurier came to us in the big room (grades 5-8) from Long Prairie, Minnesota, during my seventh grade. In the little room (grades 1-4) she enrolled her granddaughter, Arbuta Utz.

I have no idea whether she was in her fifties or sixties. Her husband was County Superintendent and she had to live up to his position as well as that of teacher of four grades. We all learned whatever was presented. There were no separate classes for fifth grade through eighth grade.

We all knew she was a descendant of John Quincy Adams; she talked about him often enough. We all knew that her grandmother was the granddaughter of John Quincy Adams, that he was a great American diplomat, that he designed the Monroe Doctrine, and that he was the sixth president of the United States.

We knew that an old Franklin heater (invented, she said, by Benjamin Franklin himself) had been in the family of the sixth president and was stored in the Utz basement.

And when John Greenleaf Whittier came calling, this old heater came out of the basement and warmed the cold feet of the world-famous poet. We all knew that she liked fishing, painting, politics, baking, books, Baptists and singing. She often told us, "Young Ladies and Gentlemen, sewing is an art. Have your mothers teach you." And yet, this lady who considered sewing an art, day after day, week after week wore a chocolate colored dress, with tucks going from the left shoulder to the hem, with a white lace collar and cuffs, white on Mondays, not so white on Fridays.

From her I learned to love reading, to love books, that the life of learning through books is exciting—and I never forgot it. And I know I passed it on to hundreds of students.

She would read to us all day long. This was her only curricula for all four grades. I was never so independent that I could read to my students all day long; one had to follow curriculum guidelines. But I could read a poem, a paragraph from a short story, a novel or a column from the newspaper to my classes every day. And I could encourage students to read their literature assignments, orally, to each other. And I knew reading books, reading almost anything, makes a difference.

It was "Grandma's" love of books, the reverence with which she handled books, that made her year with us so memorable. I remember well, we got as far as page sixteen in our citizenship books, but through her reading to us we learned citizenship. She read biographies of George Washington and John Quincy Adams and we learned his contributions as Secretary of State. We knew Lucy Stone, the nineteenth-century lecturer for women's rights, and that after her marriage she kept her name and wrote it as Mrs. Lucy Stone. And Mrs. DeLaurier approved.

She read *Oroonoko* by Aphra Behn to us; we all learned that this was a novel about an enslaved African prince whom Aphra Behn met while she was in prison in South America for chiding the lords of Parliament for making laws penalizing street women, when actually the lords most often called on these women for their own pleasure. We knew what it meant because she told us. And when a sabbatical was granted me, I went to Oxford to study her dramas and this African novel because I never forgot with what delight Grandma took it in. And she read to us from Dryden to show that we were to gather that he was inferior as a writer to Miss Aphra Behn.

I remember that so often in London I would ask about or look for markers of the Great Fire in London because I remembered the tone of her voice when she read about the fire in *The Diaries of Samuel Pepys*. As often as I've gone to Salzburg in Austria, Grandma DeLaurier went with me. I knew Mozart because she liked his music and read to us everything she could find about him—even the liners of phonograph records. I wished she could come with me to the magnificent Cathedral and listen to the compositions she loved. I can still hear her say that Mozart composed more than 600 pieces, tried to support himself but died in absolute poverty. She always said that if someone writes such fine music, society should support him. And so, in Salzburg, I visited his home, bought tapes to share with my students, and thanked Mrs. DeLaurier for reading so much about him to us.

I know that not all of us who were taught by Mrs. DeLaurier admired her as I did. I know there were those who said she disciplined with rulers; I don't remember that. There were those who said she was "too pious"; I don't remember that. Every morning and late afternoon we all sang a loud fervent Baptist *AMEN* after we sang "America the Beautiful." To me it seemed a fitting way to end the songs. There were those who said she should have taught more out of the textbooks. I didn't think so; I learned more from her reading to us. I know that most of us in the upper four grades that year, later in life, loved to travel and did travel; many of us took opportunities for further education. In West Union someone had to persuade us that both had value, and at a class reunion a few years back, we confessed it was Grandma's teaching that did it.

And I think she liked to read to us about women who made it. She read the descriptions of Ann Boleyn with relish, her false teeth clicked as she read parts she enjoyed. She even read the story of Teresa of Avila to us. With vehemence in her voice she read about Teresa standing up to Popes because Teresa was right. I remember her closing the book and saying, "And now, like Thomas Aquinas, Teresa is a great saint in her Church."

In her classroom the days went all too fast for me. She read well, and from hearing the language read well, some of us learned to write it reasonably well. We did not have anything called Geography Class, but we had maps. And no matter what we read we knew the locale of the world of the story, the essay, the poem. She taught us about dialects and we knew where and why the people of New York spoke differently than the people in Minnesota. She pointed to the map and told us where in the country people did not say Johnny Bread as we did in West Union.

She read poetry, usually following the afternoon recess, and she persuaded us to memorize some of it. Some got by with only two verses, some of us had to go for stanzas. She always made sure that the students in grade five knew what was going on, and if they didn't know what was going on, they were encouraged to put their heads on the desk as if they were going to sleep. After recess seemed to be a more difficult time for the fifth graders to concentrate. She knew many poems from memory, and when a head went down on the desk, "My heart leaps us" or "O world I cannot hold you close enough" usually had enough spirit to bring the heads back up. She loved patriotic poems, poems about nature. She especially loved "The world is charged with the grandeur of God." She recited it often and reminded us that we rural men and women surely could understand what Hopkins meant by "charged." She read poetry like an actress. When I read poetry to my classes I remembered she would tell us, "To read poetry well, you have to practice, practice."

She had some faults. While we were taking State Board Examinations, she read the answers or helped us to them. Somebody told the County Superintendent and we had to take the examinations over again. Yet we all passed!

*The St. Cloud Times* once did an article on Mrs. DeLaurier under the title, "Case of Amazing Women; Believe It or Not." To me Mrs. DeLaurier was an amazing woman, but she was more than that. She was the kind of teacher who made a difference. She shaped my life and destinies in ways I am still learning about. She gave me values about which I am still passionate and assertive. She taught me how to teach and to care about my students. What I hope I did for them is what she did for me. She took a twelve-year-old girl in a very small village and opened her eyes to the world, offering the young girl a vision and that made all the difference.

Sister Andre' Marthaler, OSB
St. Joseph, Minnesota